Jacob of Sarug's Homily on the Ascension of Our Lord

TEXTS FROM CHRISTIAN LATE ANTIQUITY

24

General Editor
George A. Kiraz

The Metrical Homilies of Mar Jacob of Sarug

GENERAL EDITOR
SEBASTIAN P. BROCK

MANAGING EDITOR
GEORGE A. KIRAZ

FASCICLE 21

JACOB OF SARUG'S HOMILY ON THE ASCENSION OF OUR LORD

TRANSLATED WITH INTRODUCTION BY
THOMAS KOLLAMPARAMPIL

GORGIAS PRESS
2010

First Gorgias Press Edition, 2010

Published in the United States of America by Gorgias Press LLC, New Jersey

ISBN 978-1-60724-141-6
ISSN 1935-6846

GORGIAS PRESS
180 Centennial Ave., Suite 3, Piscataway, NJ 08854 USA
www.gorgiaspress.com

Library of Congress Cataloging-in-Publication Data
Jacob, of Serug, 451-521.
[Homily on the Ascension of our Lord. English & Syriac]
Jacob of Sarug's Homily on the Ascension of Our Lord / translated with introduction by Thomas Kollamparampil. -- 1st Gorgias Press ed.
   p. cm. -- (Texts from Christian late antiquity, ISSN 1935-6846 ; 24) (Metrical homilies of Mar Jacob of Sarug ; fasc. 21)
Includes bibliographical references (p.   ) and indexes.
1. Jesus Christ--Ascension--Sermons. 2. Sermons, Syriac--Translations in to English. 3. Sermons, Syriac. I. Kollamparampil, Thomas. II. Title.
BR65.J283H63513 2010
232.9'7--dc22
        2010008604

The paper used in this publication meets the minimum requirements of the American National Standards.

Printed in the United States of America

This publication was made possible with a generous grant from

THE BARNABAS FUND

and

THE ATHANASIUS YESHU SAMUEL FUND

TABLE OF CONTENTS

LIST OF ABBREVIATIONS

CSCO   Corpus Scriptorum Christianorum Orientalium
ET   English translation
MHMJS   Metrical Homilies of Mar Jacob of Sarug
PO   Patrologia Orientalis

For short titles, see the Bibliography.

INTRODUCTION

INFORMATION ON THIS HOMILY

Homily Title: On the Ascension of our Lord
Source of Text: *Homiliae selectae Mar-Jacobi Sarugensis* edited by
Paul Bedjan and Sebastian Brock (Paris-Leipzig 1905,
2nd ed. Piscataway: Gorgias Press, 2006), vol. 6, pp.
196–220.
Lines: 487

OUTLINE

By his introductory words Mar Jacob awakens all human beings, the living harps of eloquent strings, to their duty of praising the Only-Begotten. The Word is hidden as well as revealed. The Word is on the throne and in the womb of Mary, hidden with the Father but revealed to us on account of us. He is the Son of God and Son of Mary, from the Most High and from below. Hence, he is ineffable. None is able to investigate or search into the exalted Word (1–60).

With the help of biblical and natural symbols Jacob of Sarug demonstrates the descent and ascent of our Redeemer who showed the way to the Father. The descent and ascent of the Son depict the Adam-Christ complementarity. The epiphany of the Son as the Sun of Righteousness was to expel all shadows of vanity and to show the way towards the Father to the world that went astray in the errors of idols. Although the Son had been smitten and had suffered in the process of bringing about restoration, he shone out with brilliance as he ascended. As the thorns were uprooted the earth rejoiced and heaven too rejoiced as he was returning to it. Both places were proud of the single Mediator and Reconciler. Error was condemned, Sheol fell down, death was bound and Adam was freed as well as the serpent bruised. With his nails he severed the bond of Eve; he received in his side the lance that had driven the household of Adam from Paradise. He restored and reconciled Adam who was in enmity with God. With his Cross

1

he opened the door of the Garden, the bridal chamber, and brought in the expelled bridegrooms (61–126).

During the forty days after the resurrection he depicted the image of the new world in the model of the birth of a male child. As an embryo becomes perfect in forty days, the Son perfected and confirmed his apostles and disciples, the organs and senses of the Good News, in order to lay hold of the whole world by proclamation. Then he led the sons of his mystery to the Mountain of Olives as if in a mystery to supply the oil for signing and giving them the sign of the Trinity for redemption. It was through the Trinity the world came into being and now the Father guards and the Son makes atonement and the Spirit sanctifies (127–224).

The Sun of Righteousness descended in the month of Kanun (December/January) and ascended in the month of Haziran (June), as the descent and ascent of the natural sun. Thus he illumined the darkened well the sins of the world and choked all shadows. Unlike Elijah who ascended by the power of the Lord in a chariot, our Lord ascended by his own power (237–274).

The Bride saw the glory of the Bridegroom, how the Slaughtered One clothed himself in power, how he subjugated death in its cave and was returning to his Father. As the truly beloved of the Bridegroom, the Bride, the Church, gathered at the mount and yearned to ascend with him. But she got the assurance that he would come again in his valiant power (275–330).

At the Ascension of the Son the different legions of spiritual beings received him in turn, each within their own boundaries, giving him honour. Beyond all of them the Only-Begotten was exalted, where not even the minds have room to be raised up. To the holy of holies, to the awesome interior tabernacle, only the High Priest, the Son, has entered (351–412). Mount Sinai served as a type of the ascension of the Son. All orders remained in the valley of the heights, as he was ascending, like the Hebrews who gathered at Mount Sinai. The people, leaders of the people, the elders and priests were allowed to ascend Mount Sinai only to particular limits. Above them all, where there was the tabernacle of the Exalted One, Moses alone entered. Similarly to the Father our High Priest, the Only-Begotten, alone entered. The High Priest alone entered with his blood to reconcile humanity with his Father. He is the offering, the High Priest and the Libation too. By descending he visited us and by ascending he redeemed us (413–486).

SUMMARY

The Praise of the Living Harp and the Eloquent Strings (1–12)
The Humility of the Unconfirmed and the Indestructible Word (13–36)
The Hidden and the Revealed Only-Begotten (37–60)
The Descent of the Son for Redemption (61–76)
The Embodied Saviour (77–110)
The Road of the Slaughtered-One to His Father (111–126)
The Perfection of the Road of Proclamation in Forty Days (127–160)
The Mystery of the Ascension from the Mountain of Olives (161–172)
The Sons of the Mystery as Witnesses to the Whole Way of the Son (173–190)
The Abiding and Sustaining Presence of the Trinity (191–224)
The Ascent of Christ, the Mediator, Reconciler and Redeemer (225–236)
The Course of the Sun and the Course of the Sun of Righteousness (237–274)
The Bride's Vision of the Bridegroom's Ascent in Glory (275–314)
The Royal Bride Consoled by the Servants of the King (315–330)
The Heavenly and the Earthly Joined in Peace (331–350)
The Son Received by the Legions on His Way (351–368)
The Ascension of the Son to Heaven (369–384)
The Accord of Honour from the Legions to the Son on His Ascent (385–412)
Mount Sinai and the Order of the Ascension of the Son (413–434)
The Entrance of the Son into the Hidden Tabernacle (435–487)

TEXT AND TRANSLATION

THE PRAISE OF THE LIVING HARP AND THE ELOQUENT STRINGS

1   O my harp,[1] be awakened for the praise of the Only-
        Begotten
    until death shall dissolve your eloquent strings.
    Give praise to the Son of God with an exalted voice
    for His praise He has appointed you;[2] why are you idle
        from praise?
5   Sing to God as long as you are alive because it is easy
        for you;
    you shall be reduced to silence, speak now, because it
        is fair for you.
    Be awakened, speak about the majesty of the Lord
        God, your Lord,
    before the sleep of death and the silence of Sheol will
        silence you.
    In the silent tomb there are neither those who praise
        nor those who speak.
10   As long as you are here, evoke praise abundantly.
    My Lord, let me not be silent from your praise not
        even when I am dead
    for anyone who lives in you on account of you, shall   John 5:24
        not die.

THE HUMILITY OF THE UNCONFINED AND THE INDESTRUCTIBLE WORD

    Wakeful is your Word and the silence of Sheol will
        not make it sleep:
    Let it [your Word] be spoken through me so that the
        coming generations shall speak it.
15   Exalted is your Word even above death, wherever it
        be,

---

[1] Cf. Hom. 165 (Presentation; MHMJS [fasc. number?]), line 293 (Bedjan V, p. 461); Ephrem, *HPar* 8:8; *HFid* 25:2–4.

[2] Giving praise is a duty, cf. *Turgomo* on Palm Sunday, 46 (ET in Kollamparampil, *Festal Homilies*, p. 277, with note 1); Ephrem, *CNis* 50:1–2; Ephrem's view of Paradise as nourishment to faith, cf. S. P. Brock, *The Luminous Eye*, pp. 78–79.

B-Br 9

196

1
5
10
197

15

because it is alive with you and the depths of Sheol do
not confine it.

Your Word, O Lord, is not confined, subject to de-
struction,

for it resembles you because regions do not confine
you.

You remained upon the throne but the womb of Mary   Ezek 1:26; Isa
was filled by you.   6:1

20   In heaven is your dwelling but on earth is your birth.

A womb contained you, a manger carried you, knees
lifted you up;

Heaven is your throne; a cave your bridal chamber,
the earth your span.

Sea is the hollow of your hand, the firmament your   Isa 40:12
sign, O Son of God!

Your power is everywhere but your glory is wrapped
in swaddling clothes!

25   Heaven is small, a virgin carries and gives you milk.

The Seraph is veiled, but Joseph is unveiled and em-   Isa 6:2ff
braces you.

You are hidden together with your Father but you are
revealed with us on account of us.[3]

For the watchers there is your fire, but for humanity
your humility.

The sound of your blessings is in the motion of the   Ezek 1:15ff
eloquent wheels

30   and the sound of your lullabies is from the lips of a
solitary woman.

Clouds are your sign, and for your mouth are drops of
milk;

on a bosom you are carried and upon the chariot you
are carried about.

Above is the Mighty One at whom the armies (of angels) tremble,

below is the Humble One mingled with the poor eve-
ryday.

---

[3] Cf. Hom. 49 (Transfiguration; MHMJS 8), lines 27–30 (Bedjan II, pp. 348–9); Hom. 18 (Palm Sunday; MHMJS 3), lines 35–38 (Bedjan I, pp. 446–7).

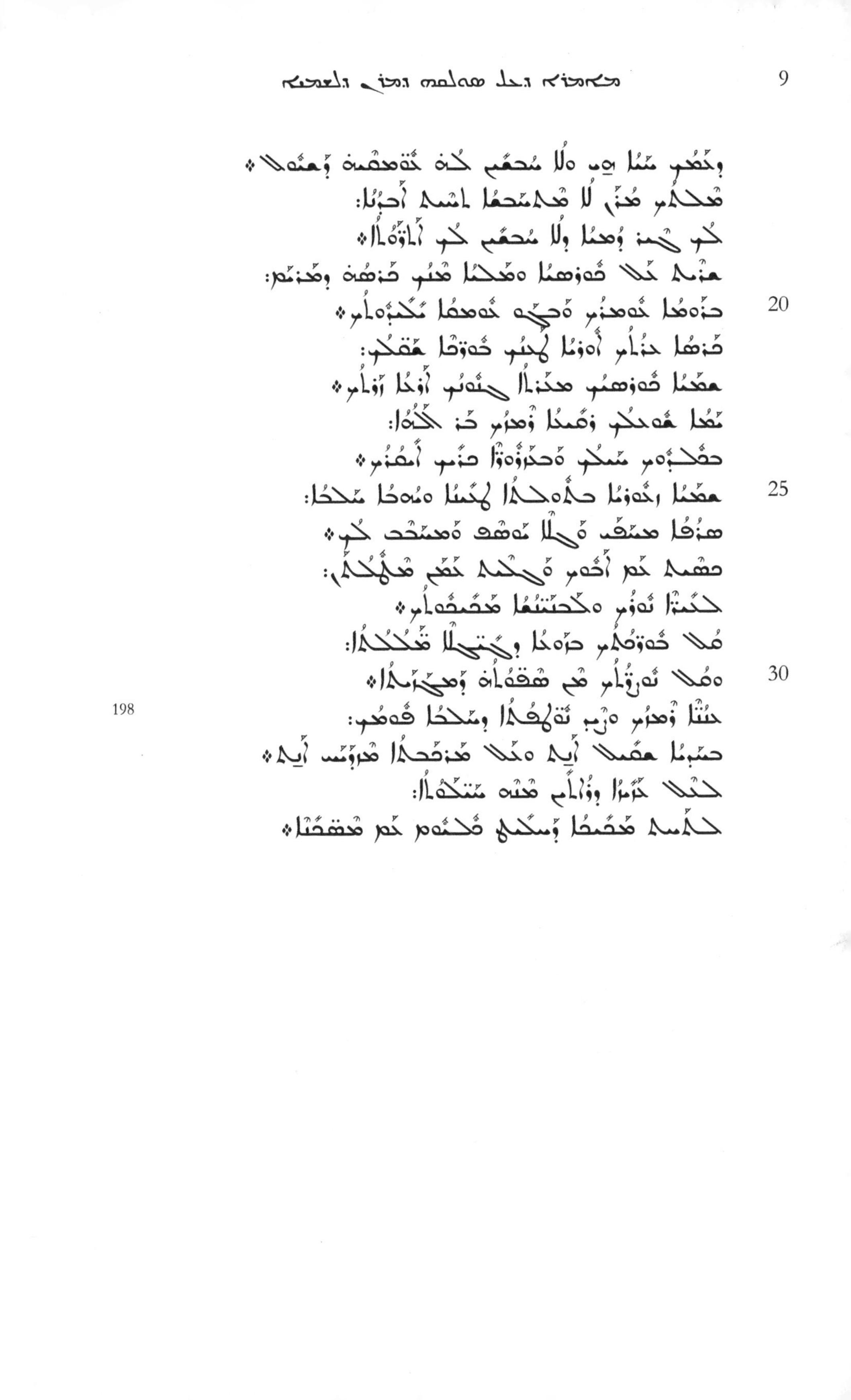

35   In heaven awesome, on the earth beloved and who is
       equal to you?
     You are hidden as well as revealed; how can anyone
       be competent to speak [of you]?

THE HIDDEN AND THE REVEALED ONLY-BEGOTTEN

The eloquent were in an uproar, the Scribes disputed
  over you; 'the wise' were defeated;
The fishermen conquered and the untaught became
  brilliant in your proclamation.
You are the Son of God, you are the Son of Man and
  you are Son of Mary

40   You are the Son of the Most High and among the
       beings below you are incomprehensible.
     You came from the height, shone out from the depth,
       you came from the Father.
     You acquired for yourself a mother, you became a
       babe, and who can investigate you?
     Hidden is your fire, revealed is your appearance, ex-
       alted is your revelation.
     Let mouths tremble and not dare to investigate you.

45   The mouth is abundantly empowered for the praise of
       you;
     and it is not easy to search into you, how you are, the
       Son of the Lord of all.
     Who shall dare to overthrow the fire of burning coals?   Isa 6:6–8
     Who will lay hold of the drops of rain to reckon
       them?
     Who is able to leap across the Sea, to leap over the
       dry land,

50   To explore the depth or to set about for the meas-
       urement of the height?
     Who is capable to set his path upon the cloud
     and to walk on it unto the limit of the Only-Begotten?
     Who has laid hold of fire in his hands, the wind in the   Prov 30:4
       palm of his hands,
     and by his fingers seizes the breezes to set them in
       order?

55   Who is the one who knows how to bind fast water   Prov 30:4
       within a veil

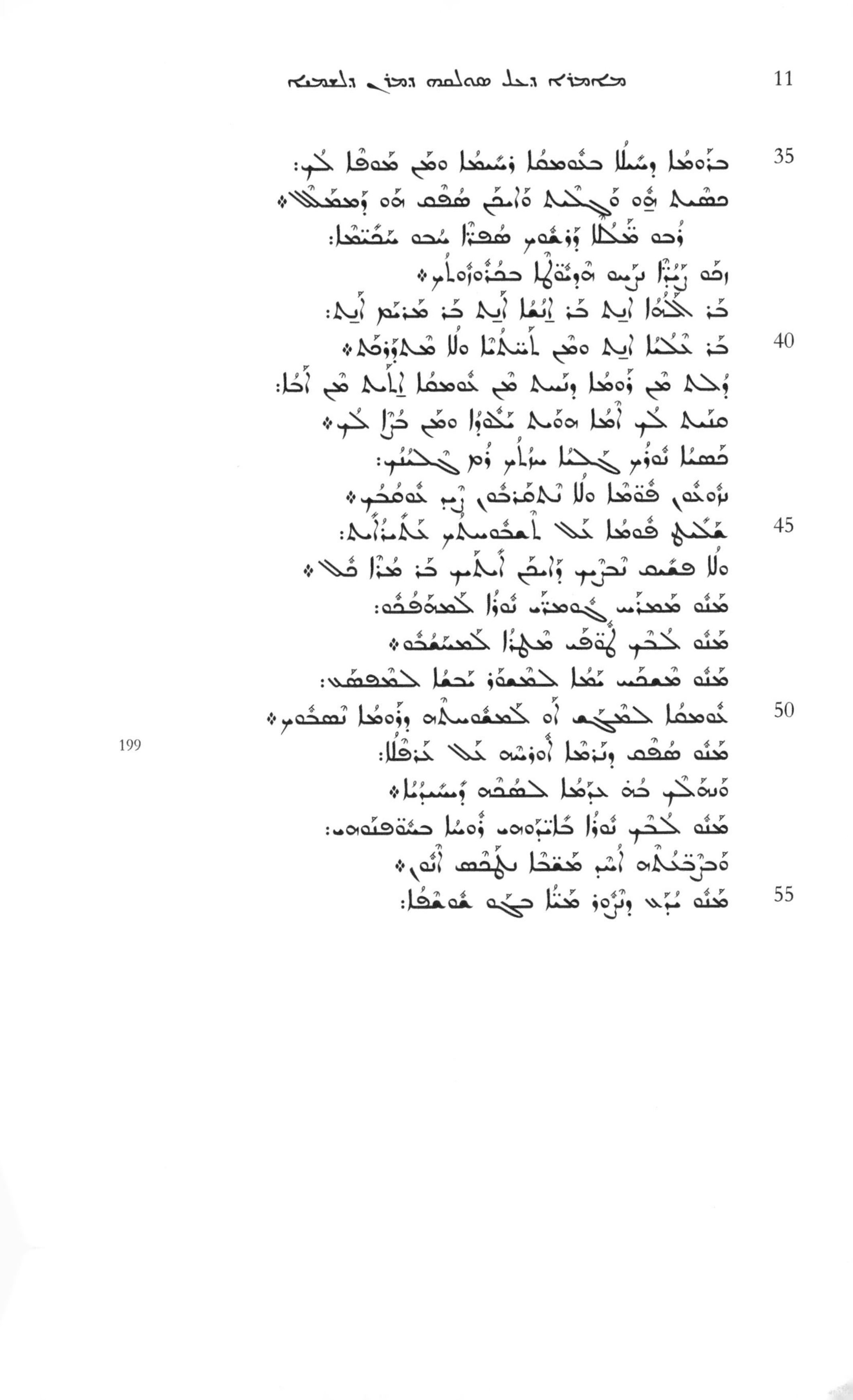

and to enclose and to contain the light of the Sun in
    his arms?

Who shows the path of a ship between the waves   Wis 5:10

and over the air the way of the eagle as well as its   Wis 5:11
    steps?

Who is indeed foolish enough to investigate the way
    of the Only-Begotten?

60   because not even the lightnings of flame approach
    Him.

THE DESCENT OF THE SON FOR REDEMPTION

He manifested His epiphany in the whole world as the
    day

and the whole creation was enlightened by Him so as
    to sing praises.

He came out as the Sun of Righteousness upon the
    regions;

and expelled from them all shadows of vanity.

65   In His going forth He showed the way to the world
    that had gone astray in the error of idols, and He
    drew

it [the world] to come to His Father.[4]

He became a great Nisan[5] that is full of glory for the
    earth,

and as blossoms, He set forth healings for the af-
    flicted.

He descended as rain and the dead quivered like   Cf. Ps. 72:6
    plants

70   and they rose up on the earth with great trembling
    from their graves.

He walked and came upon the road of the serpent,
    which [*the road*] was bitter

---

[4] Cf. Ephrem, *HFid* 62:3 (Christ, the way to the Father).

[5] The month *Nisan* (corresponds to the month of April) is a symbol of Christ, the Saviour. It is in the month *of Nisan* after the winter (which is the sign of death, captivity and the lack of fruits) the whole creation rejoices with flowers and fruits, which signify the new life and salvation in the resurrection of Christ; cf. Ephrem, *HRes* 3, 4, 5; *Crucif* 1:2; 7: 1–3; *Azym* 18; *HEcc* 51:8. Cf. Ephrem's commentary on Exodus 12:2–3; S. P. Brock, *The Luminous Eye*, p. 109.

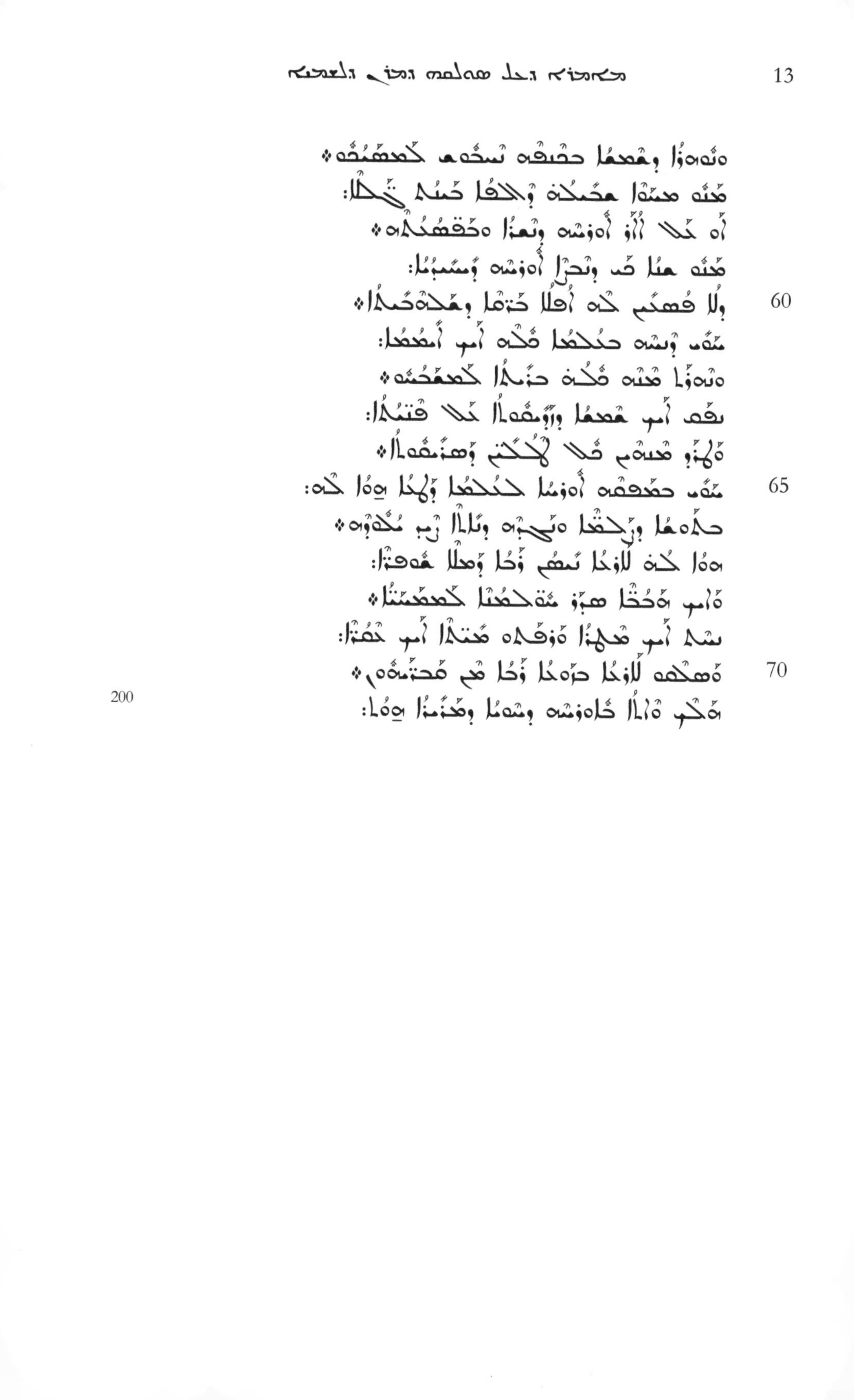

and poured out and filled it with sweet honey by His
    steps.

He entered through the ear,[6] came out from the   Isa 11:8
    womb and became a babe

and with the basilisk He played, as it is written.   Isa 11:8

75   He stretched out His hand to the hole of the asp, the
    corrupter,

and effected the return of Adam who had been bitten
    and was worn out there.

The Embodied Saviour

He became embodied that He might become capable
    of suffering

and He carried away the iniquity of the world by the
    sufferings of His crucifixion.

He brought freedom for the race of slaves that was
    enslaved

80   and He made them ascend until they became sons of
    His Father.

He went out as a Physician to the wounds (inflicted)
    by the accuser

and He drove away the sickness from humanity by
    (His) healing.

He healed the sick, He cured diseases, He cleansed the   Cf. Matt 11:4–
    lepers.   6.

He opened (the eyes of) the blind, made the bent
    straight, made the deaf hear.

85   He called the sinners, made the publicans righteous   Gen 3:23
    and brought in those driven out.

He gathered the scattered, purified the defiled and
    vivified the dead.[7]

He walked on the earth and sprinkled mercy and filled
    (it) with hope

---

[6] Syriac tradition speaks of the Word entering through the ear of Mary. This is
in sharp contrast with Eve's hearing of the serpent, the consequences of which
were undone by the wise hearing of Mary; cf. Ephrem, *HEcc* 49:7.

[7] Another manuscript has: "those gone astray have returned because He made
the publicans righteous; those far away have come, the darkened ones were illumined and the dead became alive."

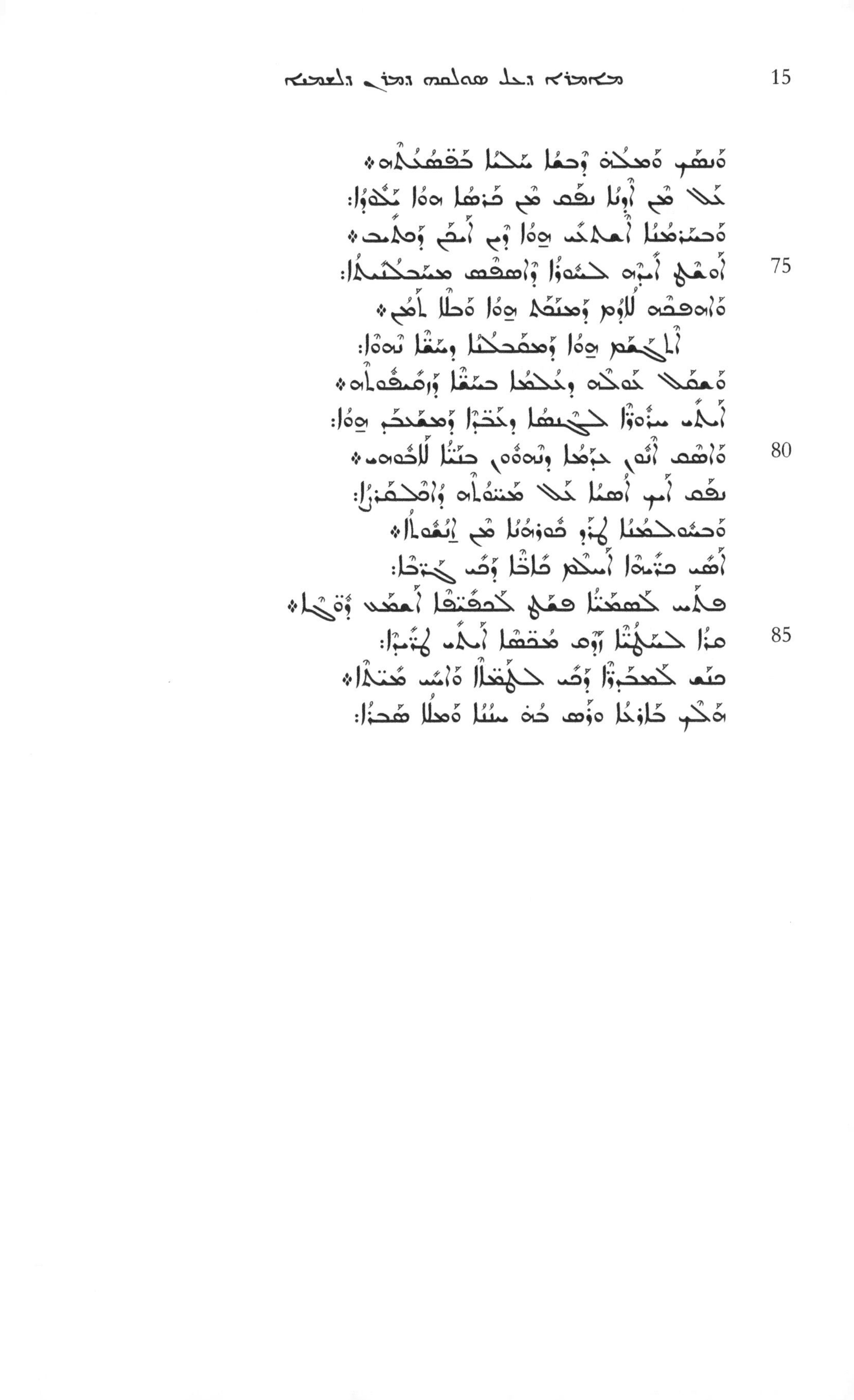

and He made peace between the earthly and the heav-
    enly beings.

He silenced and made an end to the strife which the   Gen 3:15
    serpent had set up

90   and reconciled Adam who had been at enmity with
    God.

With His Cross He opened the door of the garden,
    the beautiful bridal chamber;

and He brought in and set in it the lovely bride-
    grooms[8] who had been expelled.

He received in His side the blade of the lance of that   John 19:34
    guard;

and dismissed it to set it aside so that it would (no   Cf. Gen 3:24
    longer) drive away those of the household of
    Adam.

95   With His nails He tore into pieces that bond of Eve,   Cf. Col 2:14
    our mother,

and repaid her debt as well as raised her head that was
    bent by it [*the bond*].

By His death He descended to the abyss of the dead
    which devoured Adam.

Like a courageous Diver He brought up the pearl.

He descended, groped around the depths, visited the   Cf. 1 Pet 3:19
    buried ones, sought out the lost ones.

100   He slept near the dead and laid His couch among the
    departed.

There He made a discourse of judgement with the
    ruler,[9]

and He demanded from him the image of Adam   Cf. Matt 16:18
    which had been corrupted.

He had descended to the lowest parts of the earth to
    seek there

the superb image of the creative power that had been
    wasting away in Sheol.

---

[8] Usually the title 'Bridegroom' is reserved for Christ. But here all the redeemed are called 'bridegrooms.' Probably it alludes to the perfect likeness of
Christ achieved by the redeemed.

[9] Here 'ruler' refers to death and the evil one.

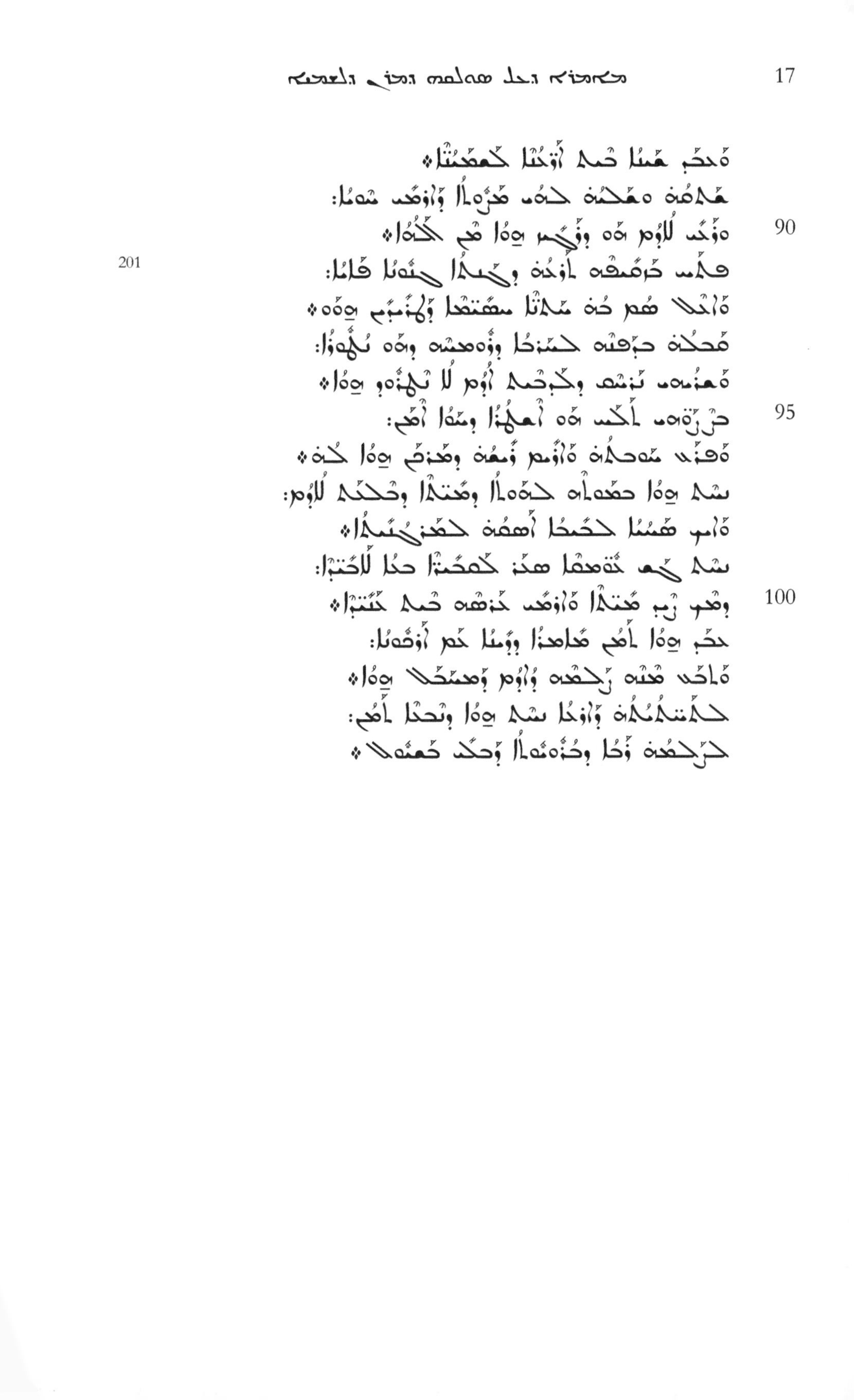

105   He contended with death in the region of death and
demanded His image;

then He carried off His own and returned to come
(away) from perdition.

He conquered the tyrant there in his place and
searched out his treasures;

and brought out the booty which was stored by him
in his castle.

He liberated the prisoner and bound the captor with
force

110   and He returned to ascend to the place of His Father   Gen 49:24
like a Mighty One.

THE ROAD OF THE SLAUGHTERED-ONE TO HIS FATHER

He set His way to return to the heights towards His
Father

and the gates of Sheol did not withstand Him when
He was coming out.

He called out in the large place of the dead and its
walls fell down[10]

and He led away the captives and guided them and   Cf. Eph 4:8
came out from perdition.

115   He ascended from slaughter and heroism cleaved to
Him;

He effected redemption and His bow[11] returned to
come with strength.

He sprinkled resurrection upon the departed and consoled them

and ascended, became brilliant from the depth with
great wonder.

Watchers met Him at the door of the tomb when He
was going out.

---

[10] Fall of Jericho is a type of the fall of Sheol.

[11] Here the reference is to OT deliverances: cf. 1 Sam 2:4 Song of Hannah for
the child Samuel; 2 Sam 22:35 the so called David's hymn of victory; Gen 49:24
Jacob's blessings; 'the bow of Christ' destroyed 'the bow of death,' cf. line 230 below.

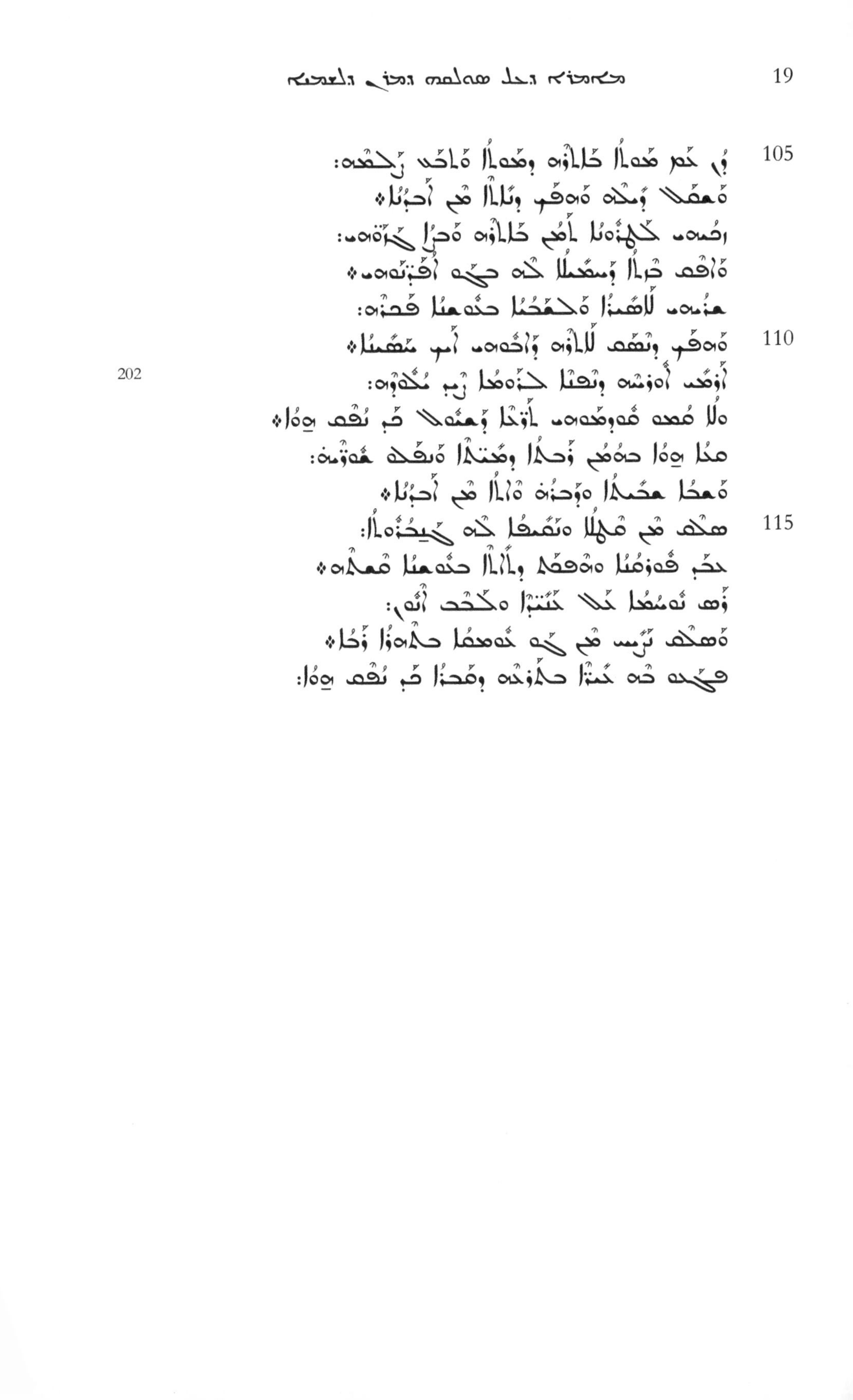

وِ : 105

120   The servants of His Father who had been sent, eagerly
           met and worshipped Him.
        The disciples, sons of the Day (light) who had been
           scattered gathered,
        and the light gladdened the female disciples who were
           sorrowful.
        The great Sun of Righteousness ascended from the
           earth
        having descended and visited all the depths and then
           He was raised.
125   He showed himself that He went and came (back)
           valiantly
        and He had visited His own and He did not bring in
           the way at His feet.[12]

THE PERFECTION OF THE ROAD OF PROCLAMATION IN FORTY DAYS

Forty days after He had come from the Resurrection   Acts 1:3
He remained on earth and then He was raised towards
        His Father.[13]
The Bridegroom who is from the tomb did not seek
        to be raised to the region of His Father,
130   until He had confirmed them about His resurrection.
        For (in) forty days He depicted the images of the new
          world
        and this is the mystery and type of she who gives birth
          to a male child:[14]
        In forty days He gathers the fetus in the womb of its
          mother
        in order to become perfect with limbs and forms.
135   And when the mansion of the soul in all forms is
          completed

---

[12] 'Bringing one's way back at his feet' means lack of success, cf. also Ephrem, *Comm. Diat.*

[13] For bridal imagery in Jacob, see Kollamparampil, *Salvation in Christ*, 229–38, 345–7.

[14] Cf. Book of Jubilees 4:9, based on Lev 12:2–5. The allusion is to the creation of soul in embryo for a male after forty days and for a female after eighty days.

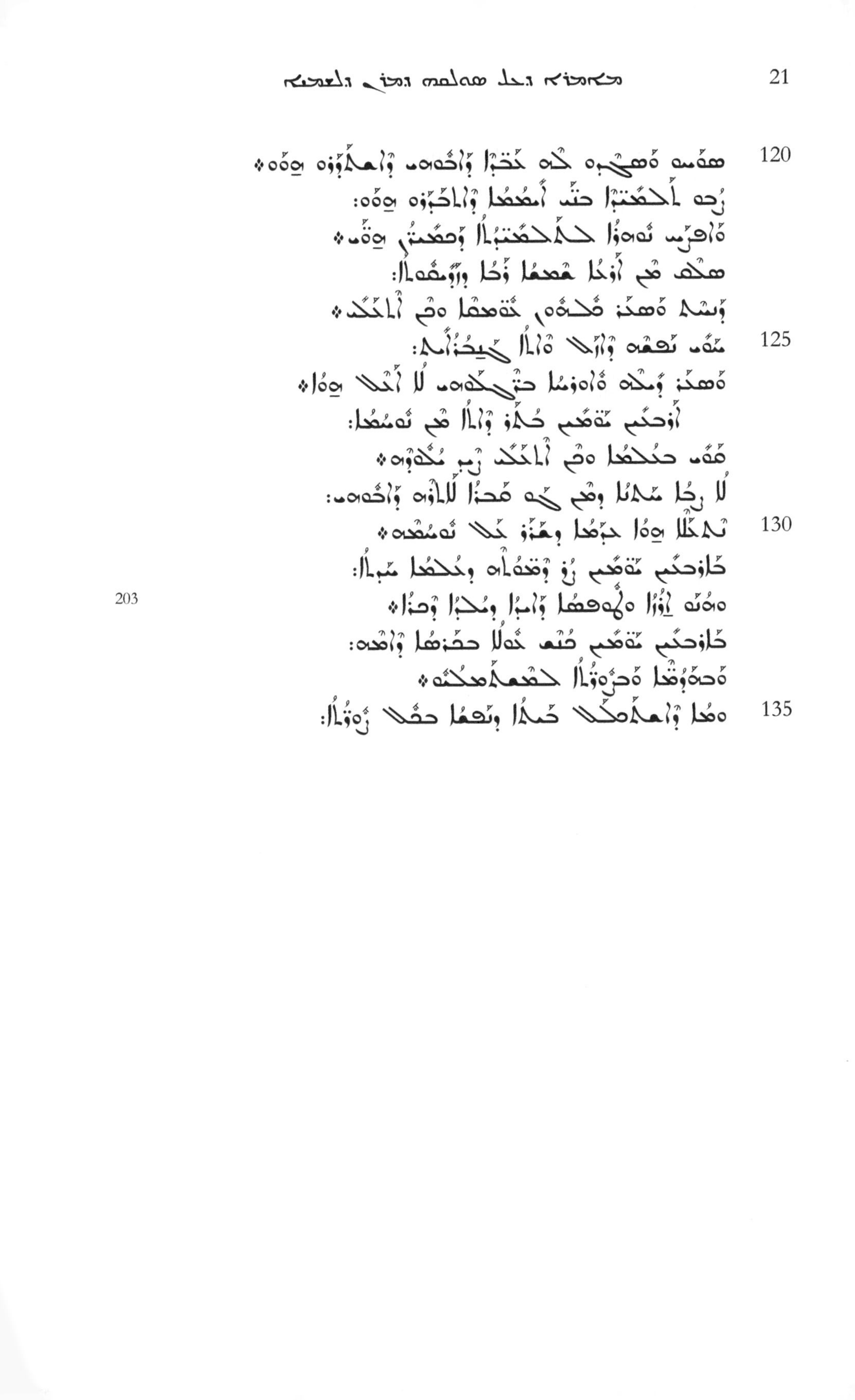

with the soul and the body it is moved consciously.
In forty days in which the embryo becomes perfect,
the Son of God perfected His apostles in faith.
And as the limbs of the fetus in the womb, He
    strengthened them.
140   He gathered them, formed them, and perfected them.
In forty days He perfected the way of His proclama-
    tion
and in the place of the soul He breathed the Holy
    Spirit into His apostles.[15]
Then on account of this He remained forty (days)
    after He was raised
so that with the nerves of faith He might strengthen
    the Good News.
145   And He ate and drank; not because He was in need of
    food,
but to confirm (them) about His resurrection that He
    is not a liar.
He ate so that they might not look on Him as an ap-
    pearance
or as a shadow; for a shadow does not eat.
On one occasion He said, "Touch me, I am not a   Luke 24:39,40
    spirit,"
150   and after this He pointed to them the place of nails.   John 20:20, 25, 27

And again they had given Him and He ate fish and   Luke 24:41–43
    honey comb
so that by means of all these they should not be
    doubtful regarding His resurrection.
And forty days He instructed them and trained them.
He taught them and confirmed them about His resur-
    rection.
155   And as if with bones, also with tendons and limbs,
and with arteries He framed the body of the aposto-
    late.

---

[15] Cf. John 20:22; Homily "On the Priesthood and the Altar," M. Albert (ed.), "Sur le Sacerdoce et l'Autel," pp. 51–77 (esp. syr. pp. 69–70; tr. pp. 57–58, lines 49–62).

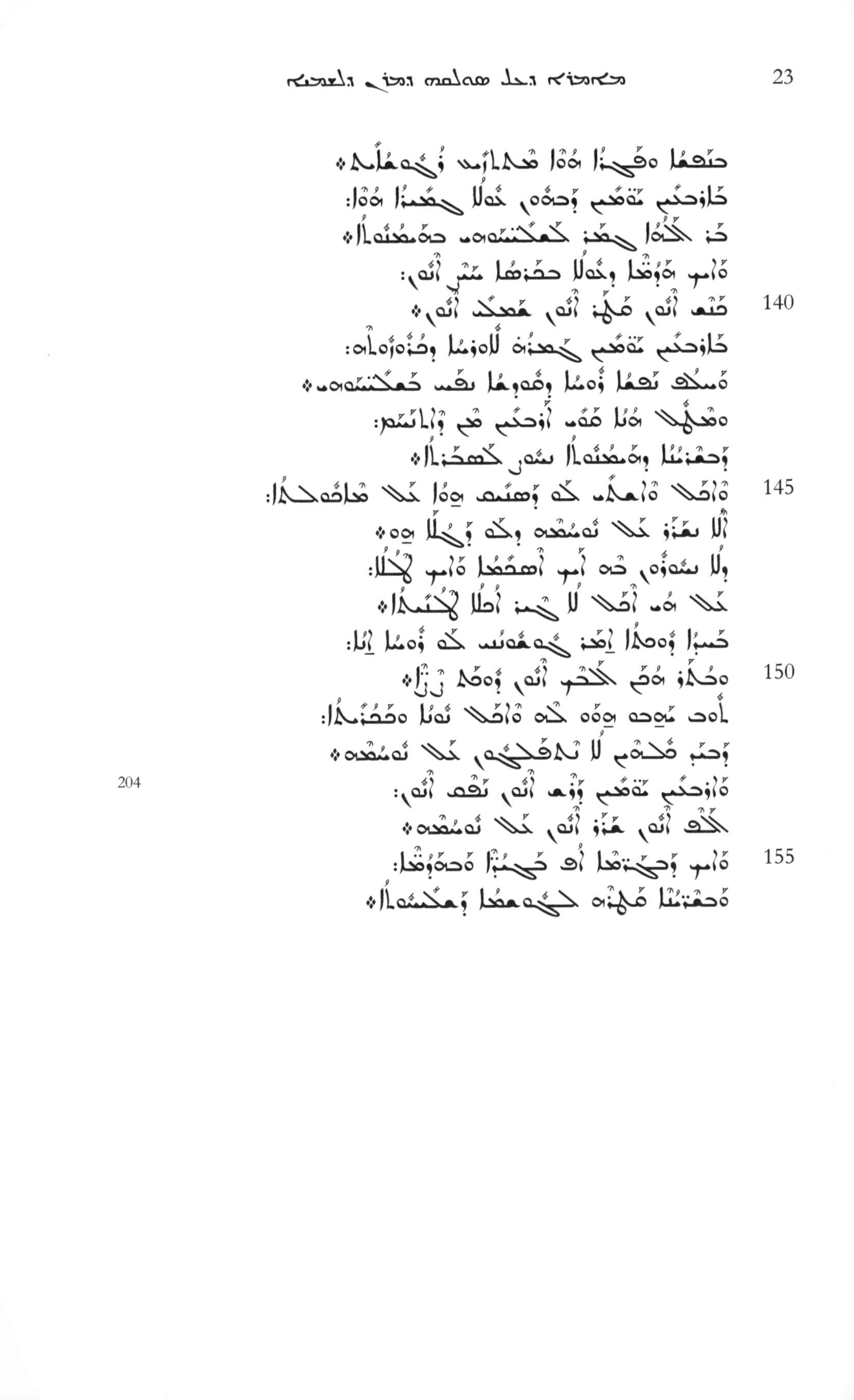

204

And when He had given perfection to the Good
    News with all its organs of the senses
and had strengthened it with all forms, as a perfect
    human being,
Then He sent it [*the Good News*] to lay hold of the
    world by the proclamation,
160   while He set His own countenance towards heaven
    above, so that He might be raised up.

THE MYSTERY OF THE ASCENSION FROM THE MOUNTAIN OF OLIVES

And to the Mountain of Olives He gathered the sons   Cf. Acts 1:6–12
    of His mystery,
because the Mountain of Olives too is a symbol of
    anointing,
for from the Mountain of Olives there shall be oil for
    Baptism;
and from it Christ was to be raised up to the place of
    His Father.
165   The treasure of oil is on the Mountain of Olives for
    anointing;
Because Christ too ascended from it towards His Fa-
    ther.
And on account of this, towards that mountain itself
    He gathered them
to supply them with the oil for the signing of the
    whole earth.
To the Mountain of Olives He gathered the Church
    for which He had died
170   so that she might see Him there as He was taken up
    to His exalted place.
The great Saviour effected His way and completed
    His deed,
and He set off to go, to send the riches to the bride
    whom He had brought (there).

THE SONS OF THE MYSTERY AS WITNESSES TO THE WHOLE WAY OF THE SON

He lifted up the poor, barren, and smitten woman
and set for her the contract that He would send forth
    to her the treasures of His Father.

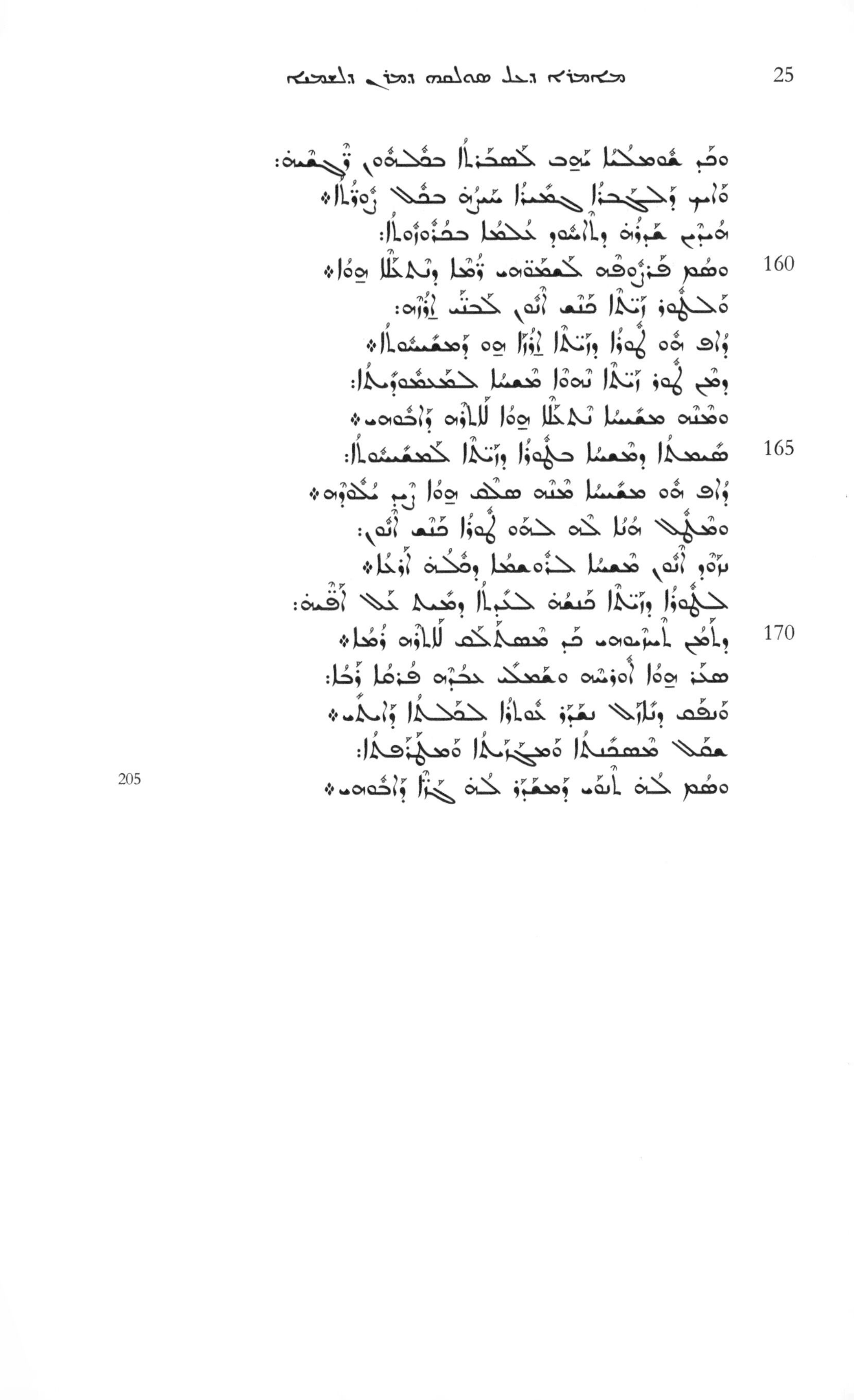

175   He had captured the captives and led them and came
        (away) from the stumbling blocks
    and gave gifts to the weary woman [the Church] who
        was needy.
    She turned away from captivity and became an apos-
        tle, and He ascended and sent
    the Holy Spirit, and She [the Spirit] gave garments to
        all who were naked.
    The great captivity came to pass, which He redeemed,
        yet she had nothing
180   and He ascended to bring down treasures and riches
        to send to her.
    He came, died in our place and ascended to make us
        live in the place of His Father,
    so that through His death He might make alive the
        world which was without life.
    The disciples, apostles and friends and the sons of the
        mystery were gathered
    so that He might show himself to them in public
        when He was ascending.
185   They saw His resurrection and they were confirmed
        about His resurrection.
    And He brought them there to see His ascension too,
    So that they might be witnesses also to His rising and
        to His resurrection;
    as well as to His ascension; and that they should fill
        the earth with His proclamation.
    They heard with their ears, their eyes saw; they
        grasped with their hands.
190   They knew Him, touched Him and they became wit-
        nesses to the whole of His way.

THE ABIDING AND SUSTAINING PRESENCE OF
THE TRINITY

    He extended His hands and by His hallowing He
        blessed them
    so that by the laying of His hand the cursed earth   Gen 3:17,18
        should be blessed.
    He called the Father and commended them so that in   John 17:11
        His name

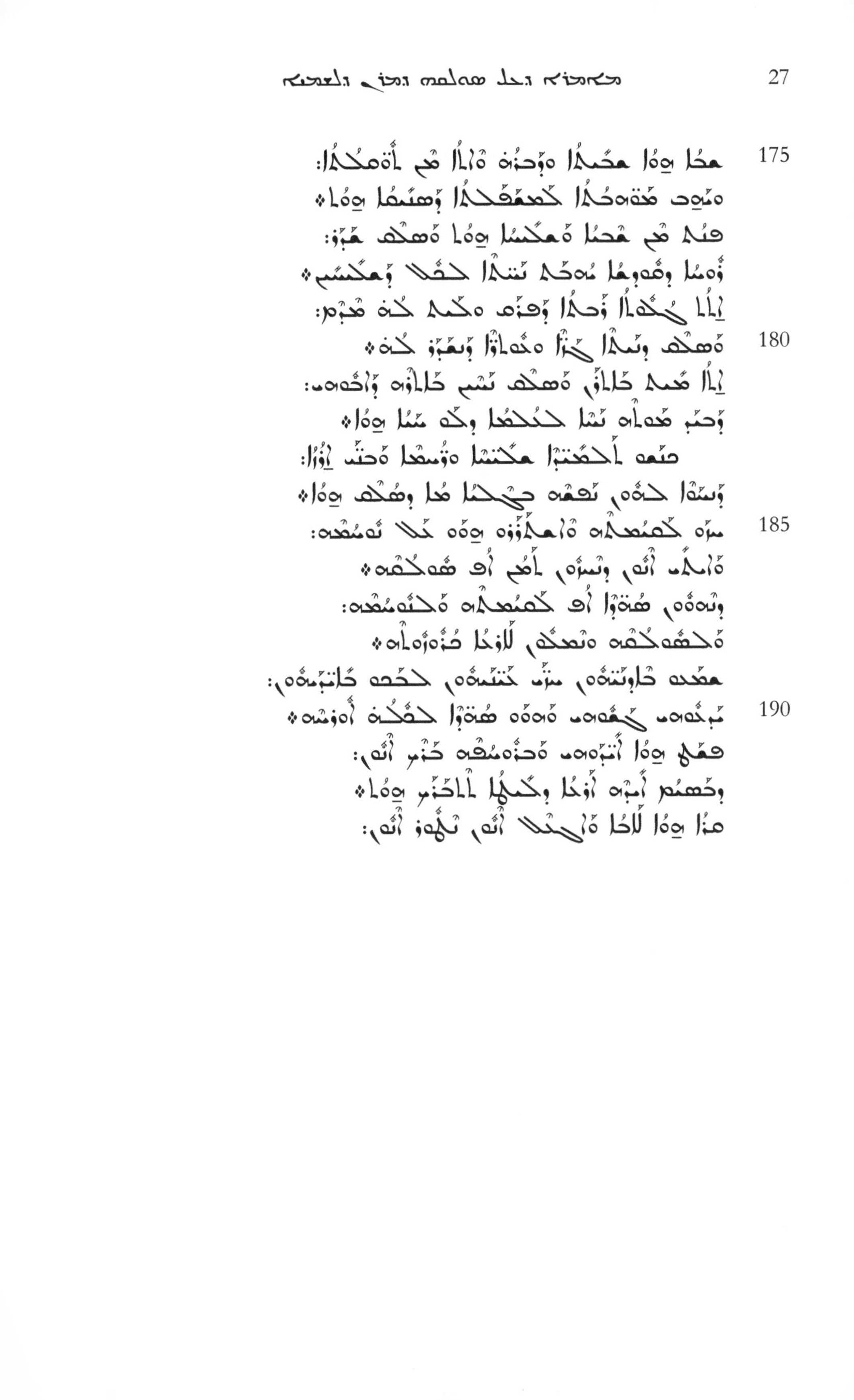

the Father might guard them from the evils of the evil world.

195   He had given peace so that they themselves might give (it) to the whole earth,   John 20:21

and He would fill them with His peace, instead of Himself.

He encouraged them and promised them, "I am with you"   Matt 28:20

so that when He would be raised up from among them it would not sadden them.

He is with them and behold, the name of the Father is with them

200   and He will send the Spirit so as not to leave them behind as orphans.   John 14:18

His peace is with them and the name of the Father was made the guard,

and the advocate carried the riches for the discipleship.

"Father, keep them in your name" for, your name is great   John 17:11

and the name of the Father accompanied the apostles by the word of the Son.

205   For, the Son said, "I am with you," and He was not lying   Matt 28:20

and He was with them as He had promised in the sight of many.

The Spirit came and He brought the riches and He was with them.

The Father and the Son and the Holy Spirit as it was foretold.

The Father who guards, the Son who makes atonement, and the sanctifying Spirit;

210   the Trinity through which the world came into being from nothing.

At that moment the world learned about the Trinity.

The hidden mysteries were made manifest and they went out to the whole world.

He taught them, He confirmed them, He sent them,

as the sun sends its radiance to the whole earth.

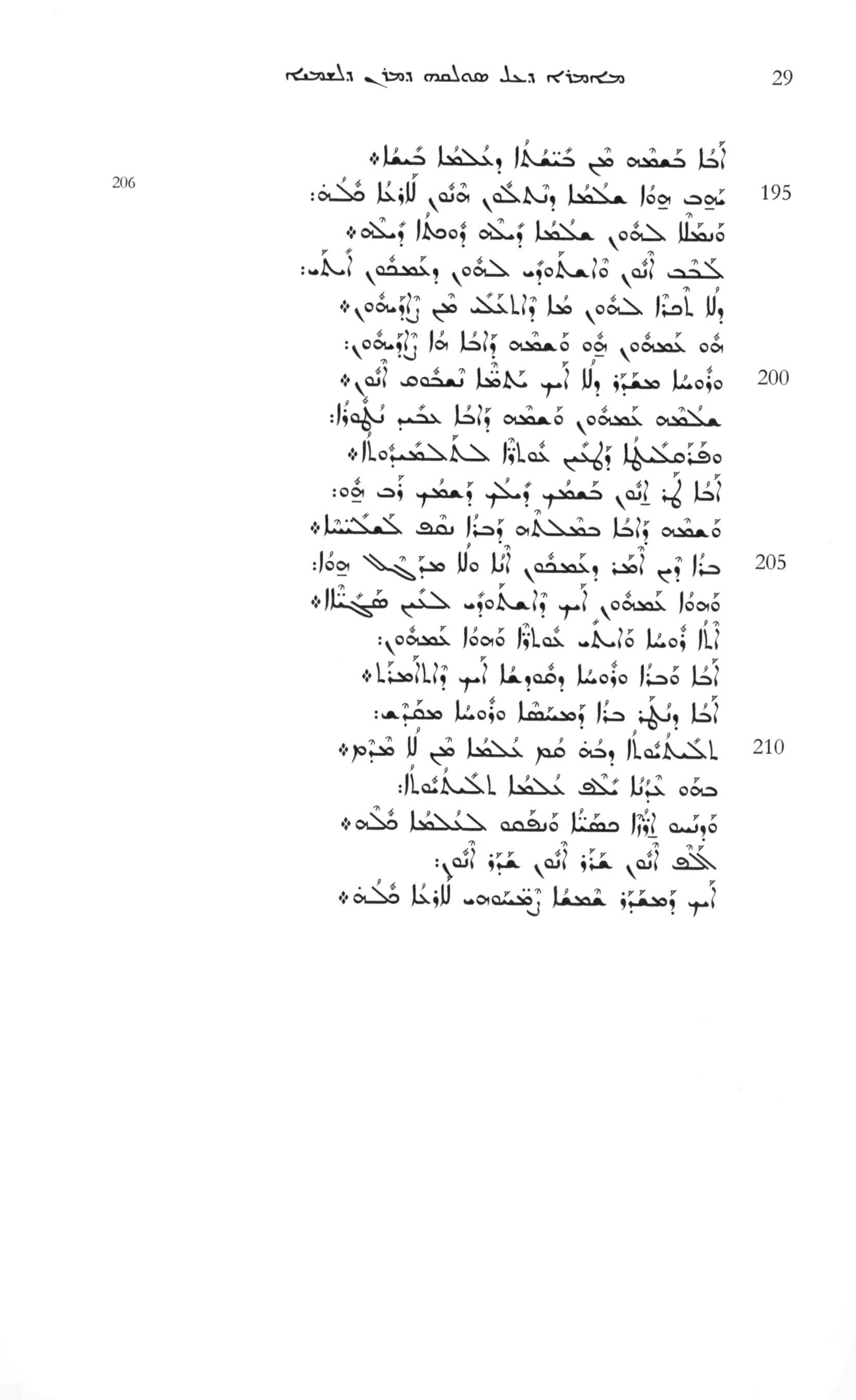

206

215 The rays went out from the globe of the great Light,
　　　following the night during which the whole creation
　　　　　was dark.
　　　He commanded them; proceed forth, go, make disci-
　　　　　ples and baptize the peoples,
　　　in the name of the Father and in the name of the Son　　Matt 28:19
　　　　　and in the name of the Spirit.
　　　The great sign of the Trinity which has no limit
220 He gave to the apostles, so that by it the peoples of
　　　　　the earth might be signed.[16]
　　　From the Mount of Olives He gave the Trinity and
　　　　　the oil;
　　　Oil for the signing and the Trinity for redemption.
　　　He commended them, blessed them, and encouraged
　　　　　them.
　　　He equipped them and commanded them to preach.

THE ASCENT OF CHRIST, THE MEDIATOR, RECONCILER AND REDEEMER

225 While they were looking at Him He was raised from　　Acts 1:9
　　　　　among them;
　　　and the heights received Him while adoring Him with
　　　　　their crowns.
　　　He ascended in glory and mounted strength and
　　　　　(manly) power;
　　　the heights and the depths were rejoicing in Him who
　　　　　reconciled them.
　　　(He was) smitten while redeeming, suffered while re-
　　　　　storing; He ascended while being brilliant
230 and exalted is His bow and He is both feared and glo-
　　　　　rified above (other) redeemers.
　　　The earth rejoiced because He uprooted its thorns　　Gen 3:17,18
　　　　　and then He was exalted.
　　　Heaven rejoiced because the Lord of the heights sol-
　　　　　emnly came to her.
　　　Both places were proud of the unique Mediator who
　　　　　reconciled them,

---

[16] Cf. *HFid* 13:5.

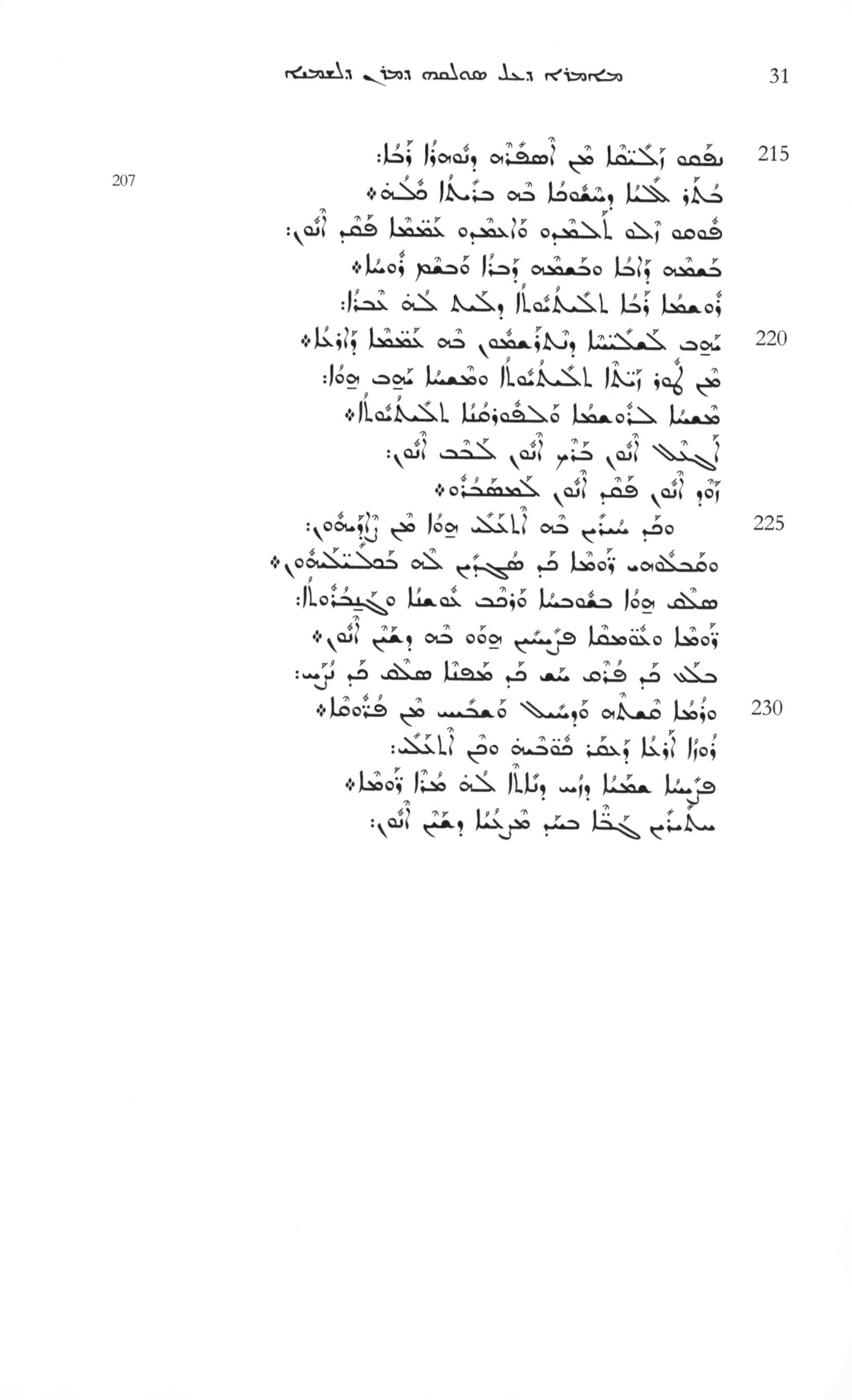

for He reconciled heaven and earth, which were at
    enmity.

235 Error was condemned; sin fell down and Sheol was
    overthrown,

death was then bound, Adam was then freed, and the   Gen 3:15
    asp was bruised.

THE COURSE OF THE SUN AND THE COURSE OF THE SUN OF RIGHTEOUSNESS

Light reigned and darkness came to an end from the
    regions.

The Day conquered and choked the night from hu-
    manity.

The sun ascended and remained in its higher degree,

240 and it shortened the extended shadows and destroyed
    them.

He [Jesus] descended in Kanun[17] as also the sun de-
    scends in degrees.[18]

He ascended in Haziran[19] and by His light He choked
    darkness.

In the month of light in which sun ascended to the
    high degree;

in it the luminary Son too was exalted to the height.

245 In this month which is at the top of that vault of the
    firmament,

the sun stands and looks forth to see all fountains.

In that (month) the great Sun of Righteousness was
    exalted,

and all the depths that were darkened were illumined
    by Him.

The sun gazes into the well in Haziran and it illumines
    the well too;

250 for, in that (month) it [the sun] is exalted and lays hold
    of the extremes by means of all its degrees.

As far as the sun would go up, it ascends to the
    heights above.

---

[17] The period of December-January.

[18] Cf. *Turgomo* on Nativity, 22 (ET in Kollamparampil, *Festal Homilies*, p. 135).

[19] The month of June.

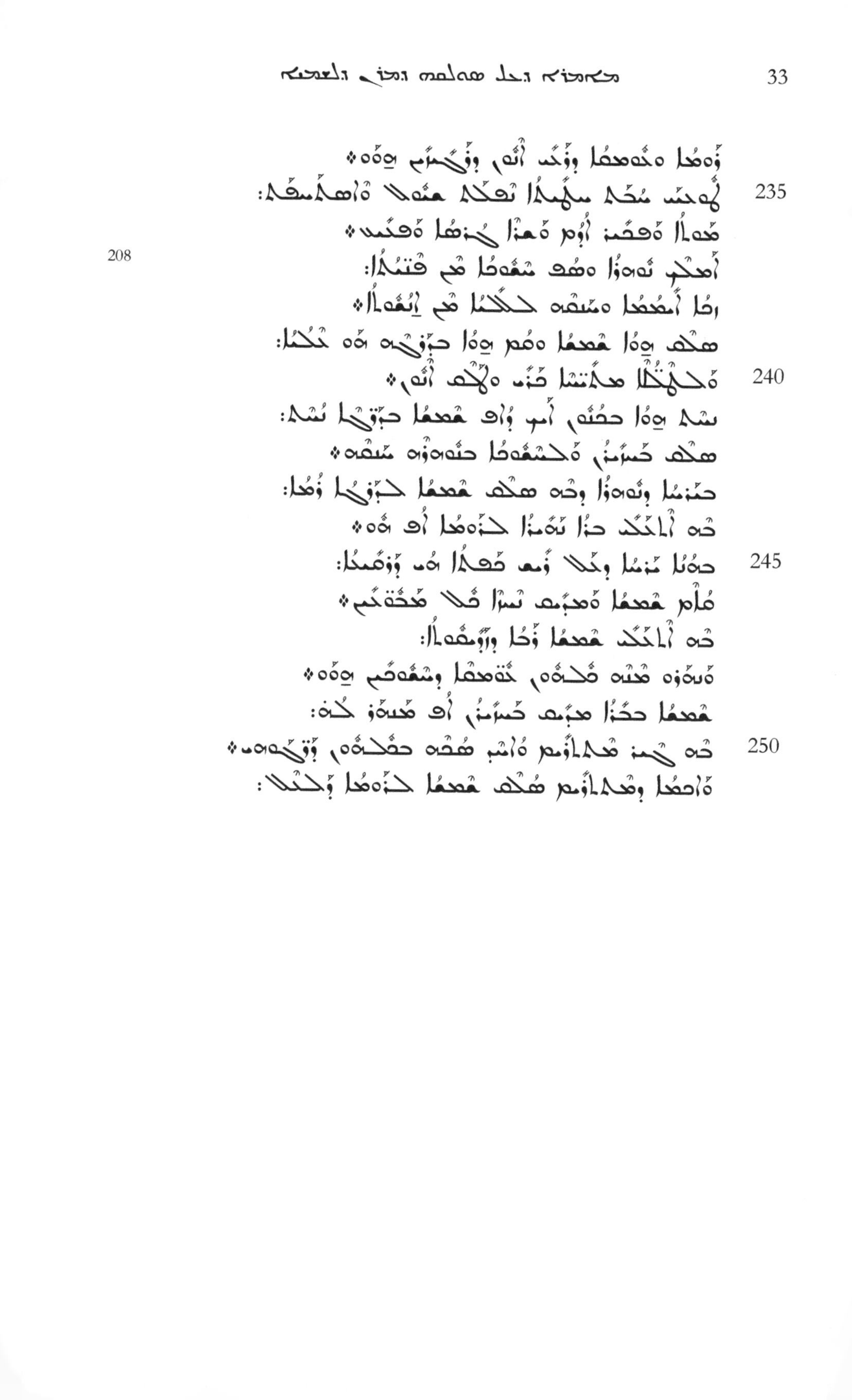

208

Thus its light shines forth, descends to the depths that
   are below.

The sin of the world was like a well[20] that was dark   Gen 29:10

and when our Sun was raised to the height, His light
   shone forth into it.

255   He was exalted and His light descended and choked
         the shadows;

and He shortened them, put an end to them; He made
   them vanish.

The sun depicts the descent and ascent of the Son of
   God,

in the course of its way to the one who sees clearly.

In (the month of) Kanun is His birth and in it the sun
   too was brought low

260   as it proclaims that the luminary Son descended to the
         earth.

Again in (the month of) Haziran the sun ascended on
   its way

and it depicts the figure of the Light, the Messiah who
   was exalted in it [Haziran].

The manifestation of the Son of God reigned upon
   the regions

and cut off the gloomy shadows which were spread
   out.

265   He was exalted from the Mountain of Olives as it is   Acts 1:12
         written.

He was raised up; not that someone raised Him when
   He was ascending.

It was not a chariot, as of Elijah, that descended after   2 Kgs 2:11
   Him.

For, regarding Elijah, when he was ascending, the
   Lord made him ascend.

And with a chariot and horses of fire He made for
   him a solemn procession;

---

[20] 'the well of sin'; the stone which Jacob removed from the well (cf. Gen.
29:10) was a type of the 'sin of the world' removed by Christ, cf. Bedjan III (Hom.
75), p. 213, lines 1–10; Bedjan III (Hom. 80), p. 310, lines 13–16.

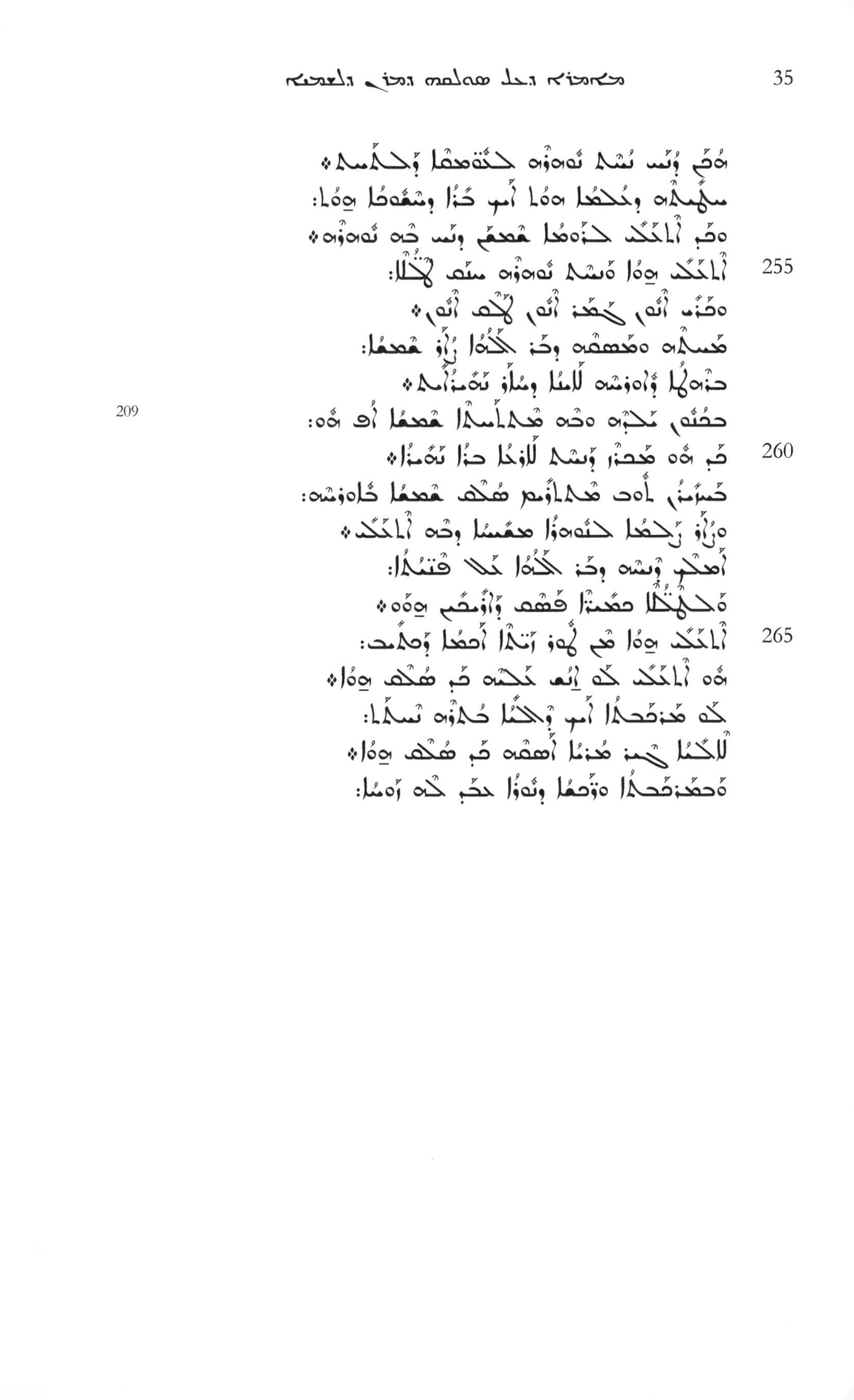

270 because he was not able to ascend by his own power
     to where he ascended.
For our Lord was exalted as it is written
and no conveyance was needed for Him when He was
     lifted up.
The son of the sojourners needed to mount because
     he was a human being;
but the Son of God did not seek a conveyance be-
     cause He was God.

THE BRIDE'S VISION OF THE BRIDEGROOM'S ASCENT IN GLORY

275 The glorified Bridegroom was exalted to the place of
     His Father,
and the band of the children of light became agitated
     upon His departure.
The bride saw the Bridegroom in glory as He was as-
     cending,
and her head, which had been bent downwards when
     He suffered dishonour, was lifted up.
She perceived Him who mounted on power and as-
     cended to His Father

280 and the heart of her, who had suffered reproach on
     account of His death, was relieved.
She perceived the Slaughtered One who clothed him-
     self in power and was flying in the air
and she forgot all the insults of the crucifixion.
She perceived the clouds and the mist that ran before
     Him
and she disregarded the mockers who were at Gol-
     gotha.

285 She perceived Him who subjugated death in its cave,
     and returned to His place;
and she went out following Him so that she may go
     with Him as the daughter of light.
She said to Him, "Draw me after you to where you
     are going.
I have become yours, let me ascend with you to your
     Father.

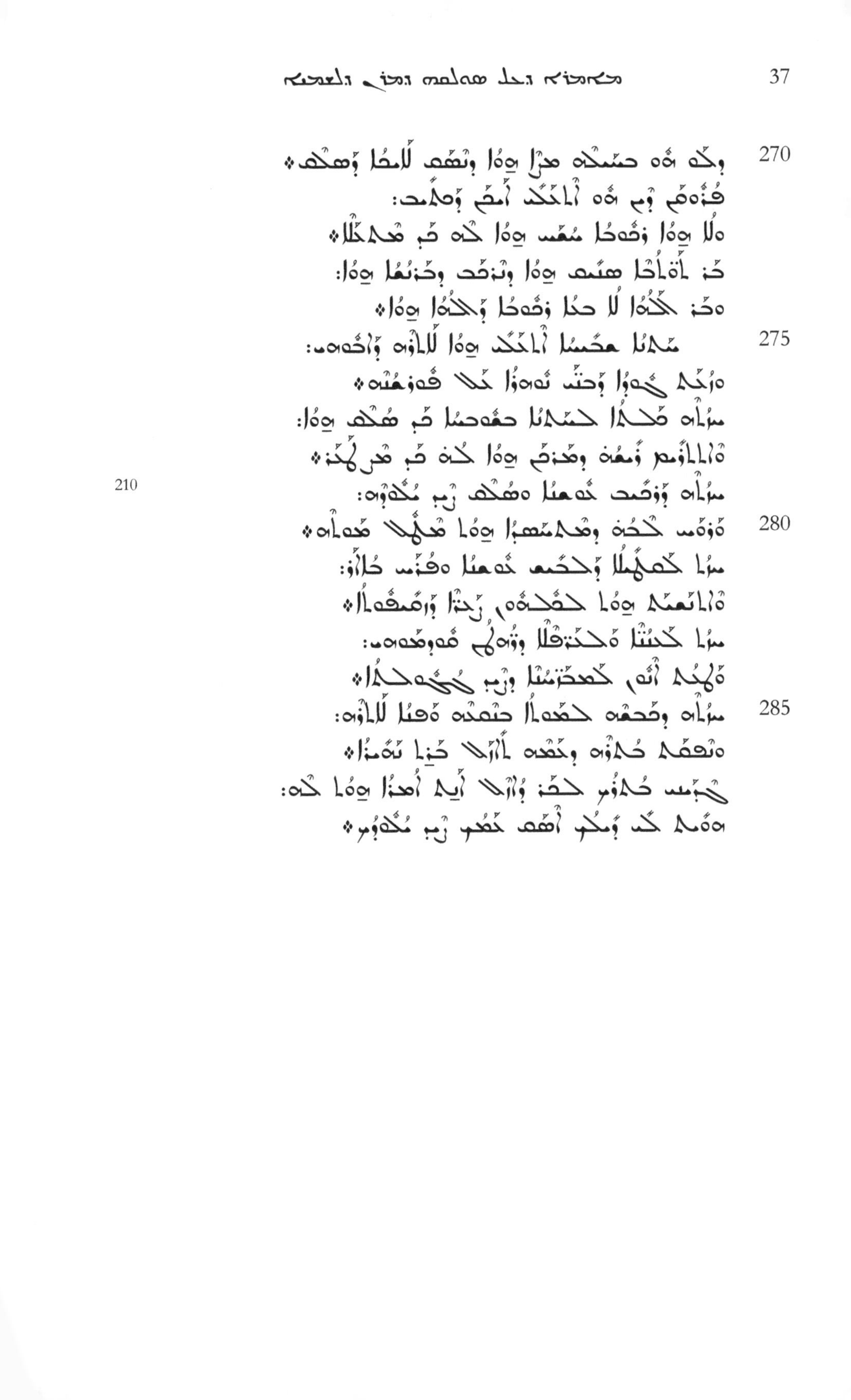

With love you sought me, with suffering you be-
trothed me, with the sword you redeemed me

290   and behold you are glorified; following you let me run
to the place of your Father.

I entered with you into the tribunal, to perceive your
dishonour.

From the Jews I have received ignominy because of
you.

I feared I might die when you were mocked on the
Cross.

I fled and concealed myself when you were beaten by
the wicked.

295   I was mocked with you when they crucified you between the robbers.

Again it pained me when they placed you with the
dead in the tomb.

I have been comforted and I forgot my sadness because of you, the Brilliant One.

Let me go with you because I am persecuted on account of you.

Let your name be for me the oil of myrrh which de-   Song 1:3
lights me,

300   for, your mercy is better than wine:[21] I shall be con-   Cf. Song 1:2
soled in you.

Let me go with you, Bridegroom, to your place because I love you.

Reckon me in your flock: I have gone astray, may I be
gathered in you.[22]

Daughters of Jerusalem, where have you seen the   Cf. Song 5:8
royal Bridegroom?

Much have I sought for Him, He ascended to his
place and I did not find Him.

---

[21] Cf. *Turgomo* on the Fast, 44 (ET in Kollamparampil, *Festal Homilies*, p. 245).
(At the ascension the bride, the Church, recognizes the mercy of God. But Adam
failed to recognize it).

[22] A similar confession of the Church is found in Albert, *Juifs*, VI, 313–44.

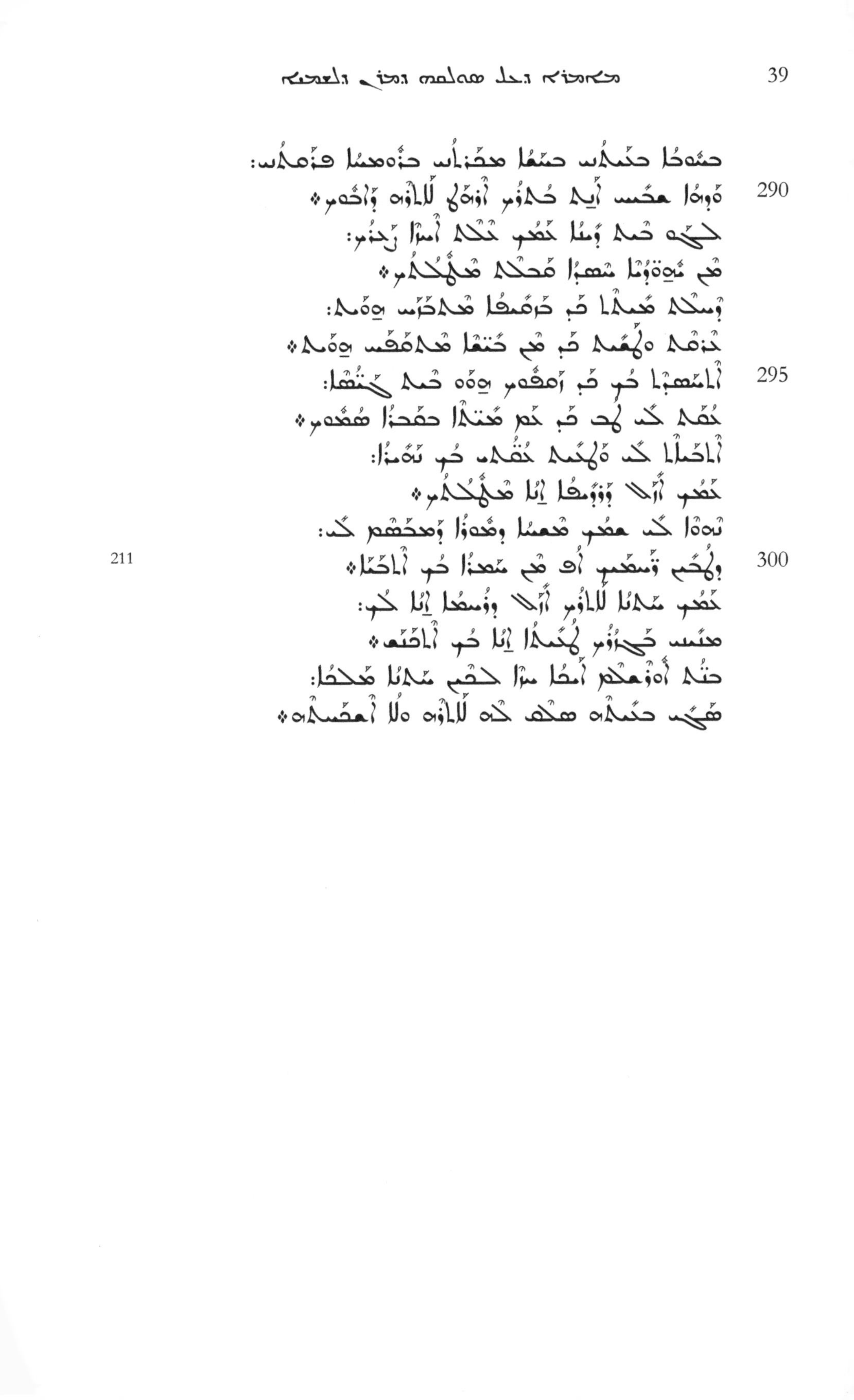

305 Behold, I am sick with the love of the Bridegroom   Cf. Song 2:5
    and I am seeking Him.
    I love Him because He is much more beautiful than
    all beauties.
    Compassion is poured out upon His lips when He   Cf. Song 5:13
    speaks.
    In His appearance He is the most beautiful of men for   Cf. Song 5:10
    the one who looks at Him.
    His garments were fragrant with the vapour of the   Cf. Song 5:1,
    incense like that of Aaron;   16
310 And the white and red that flow from Him, water and   John 19:34
    blood.   Cf. Song 4:15
    As the couch of perfumes are His cheeks to the one   Cf. Song 5:13
    who perceives Him.
    He is wholly perfume, for His Father was reconciled
    to the world through Him.
    He met me on the way but I did not recognize Him,
    for I was foolish.
    He ascended to His heaven; who shall make me as-
    cend to Him that I may see Him?"

THE ROYAL BRIDE CONSOLED BY THE SERVANTS OF THE KING

315 The company of the apostles stands upon the mount
    of Olives.
    The virgin bride then gazes at the Bridegroom who
    was raised up.
    And behold, as she was about to lament because He   Acts 1:11
    had been raised up, leaving her as He ascended,
    angels approached to console her: "Behold He will
    come."
    The servants of the King were consoling her, the royal
    bride:
320 "You should not be grieved because the same Bride-   Acts 1:11
    groom will come and you shall (surely) see Him.
    He went in order to come (back) and bring to you
    riches with Him.
    He will not leave you, He will come to you, look out
    for Him who shall come.
    In His body He carried you and behold, you are with
    Him in His exalted place,

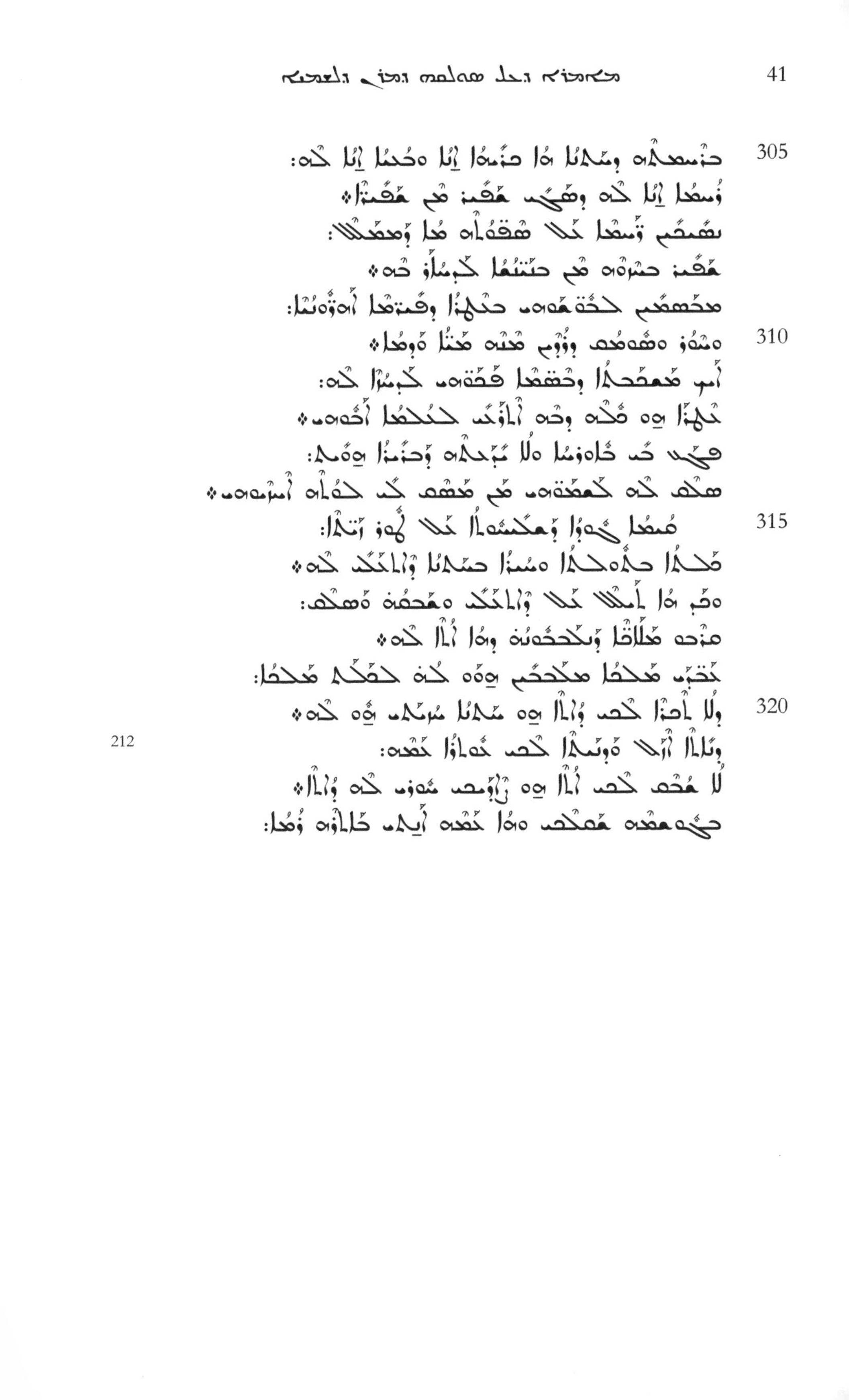

212

and He gave you His spirit and behold, He is with you
    here in your place.

325   You yourself came into being from Him, but He be-
    came from you and He will not

leave you (alone). He is one with you, He will come to
    you, do not be grieved."

Angels approached the disciples and encouraged
    them;

"your Lord will come, do not be grieved because He
    was exalted.

You have seen that He went and you will also see   Acts 1: 11
    Him when He comes;

330   and in His second coming His manly power will shine
    forth."

THE HEAVENLY AND THE EARTHLY JOINED IN PEACE

The angels came there to rejoice with the disciples.

For He had joined one party with the other in great
    peace.

Because of their joy angels clothed themselves as it
    were in white robes

because He had reconciled with them the race of men
    who were at enmity.

335   In the Son of God, heaven and earth were joined each
    other;

and in Him were pacified, both the human race and
    the angels.

The order of the heavenly beings desired to see His
    being,

because He had not been seen by them until He came
    and became embodied among us.

They were knowing Him that He is with His Father
    and hidden with Him;

340   but the heavenly hosts were not capable of seeing
    Him.[23]

---

[23] Another manuscript has: 'Because their angels see eternally the countenance of my Father who is in heaven' (cf. Matt 18:10).

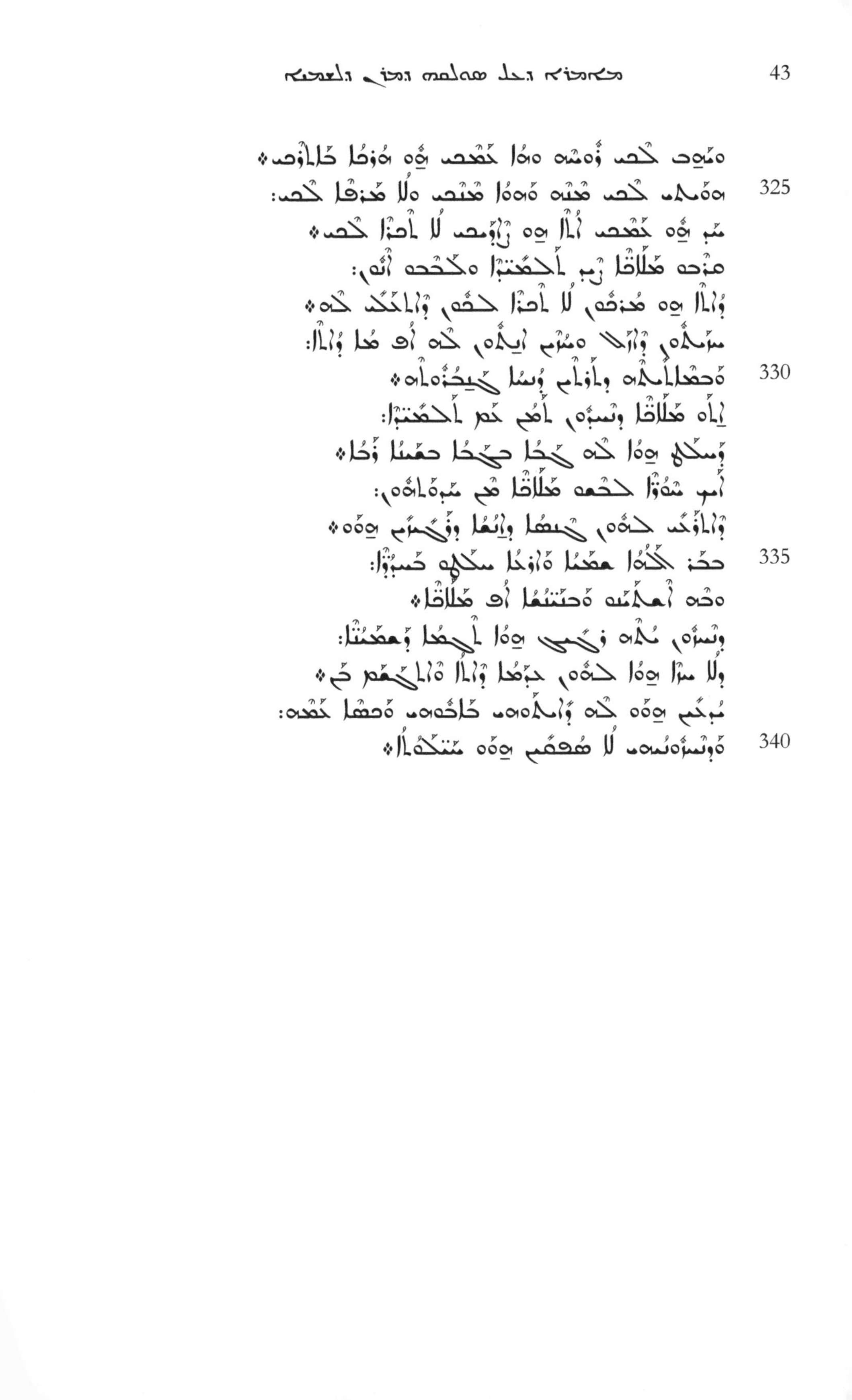

And when He descended to the earth in His love to
    come in the flesh,

the legions thronged to behold Him as He had been
    made manifest.

The powers and captains[24] with their divisions had
    marvelled,

because the Hidden One willed and became revealed
    that they might behold Him.

345   And on the way to heaven the ranks have gathered to
    see Him,

because the tidings that He had come moved them
    and they were stirred to give honour to Him.

They had earnestly desired to see the revelation of the
    Son.

A new wonder, a mystery, that He himself willed to
    reveal.

He was revealed in the flesh and in glory He ascended

350   and He was seen by men and angels when He was
    ascending.

THE SON RECEIVED BY THE LEGIONS ON HIS WAY

It is written that a cloud received Him when He was
    exalted.   Acts 1:9 (*Peshitta*)

Not that it [*the cloud*] carried Him but it did receive and
    honour Him.

He was exalted and then the cloud received Him in its
    region,

as all the (heavenly) divisions too received Him when
    He was passing.

355   In the place of babes, a babe[25] received Him because
    He came to its place;

and He came to the river and baptism received Him.

The children met Him, and they all received Him with
    their hosannas;

---

[24] It can be rendered also as 'Dominions,' 'Archangels,' etc.

[25] The reference is to John the baptist in the womb of Elizabeth; cf. *FH I 477–502.*

345
350
355

and when He was passing by the trees they gave their
    branches.

He entered in the tribunal and they honoured Him   Matt 27:28 *et*
    with scarlet robes.   *par*

360   He ascended the Cross and they wrote on it, "King"   Matt 27:37 *et*
    although they were not willing.   *par*

He decided to enter Sheol filled with the dead

and the dead of Sheol came out, and received Him as
    He was entering.

Into the tomb He had entered and the dwellers of the
    tombs came forth to honour Him

and wheresoever He went the legions of the place   Matt 27:52,53
    received Him.

365   And when He was exalted and arrived at the place of
    the clouds,

the clouds earnestly desired Him and went out for
    meeting Him, to receive Him.

The cloud did not come down to the earth, while He
    was ascending;

when He had approached towards it in its place, it [*the
cloud*] received Him.

THE ASCENSION OF THE SON TO HEAVEN

From the earth unto heaven He was exalted,

370   as the book of Luke makes known to those who dis-   Luke 24:51;
    cern.   Acts 1:9–11

And behold, when He was arriving at that exalted   Acts 1:9
    place of the clouds

the cloud proceeded, and received Him as He was
    passing.

Not that it would carry (Him), but it went out to re-
    ceive Him solemnly,

for the meeting of its Lord who had come to pass by
    its neighbourhood.

375   For the cloud did not ascend with Him to where He
    ascended;

but in its place it received Him and it stayed behind
    Him.

As He had left the earth at His ascent when He was
    exalted,

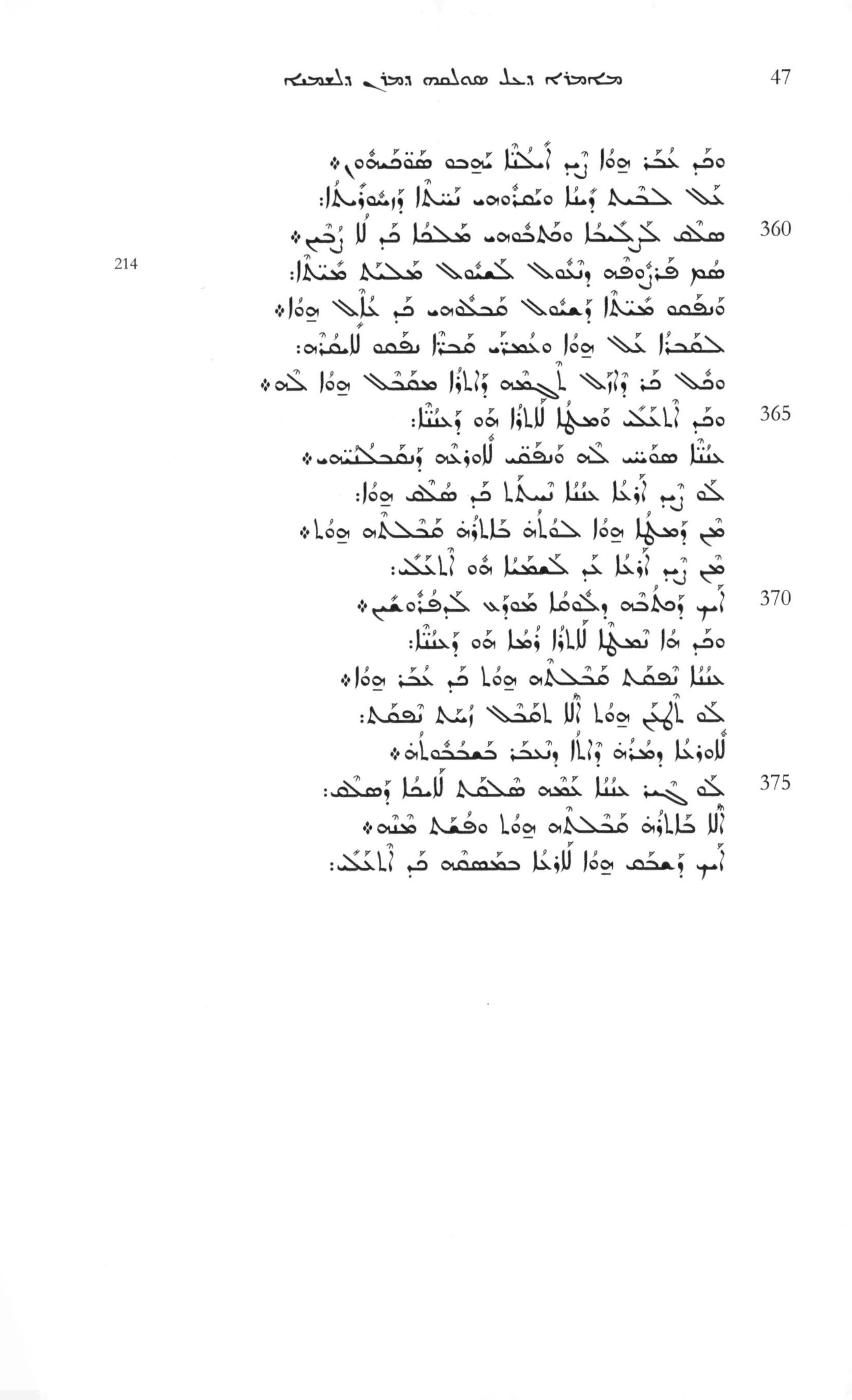

thus He left the cloud too when He was ascending.

And all the legions in their places and in their boundaries

380   were receiving Him when He was raised to His exalted place.

They were receiving Him, they did not carry Him to be exalted

because He is the One who was carrying the regions and their legions.

He left the cloud in that troubled place of the clouds

and higher than that into the serene place He was exalted.

THE ACCORD OF HONOUR FROM THE LEGIONS TO THE SON ON HIS ASCENT

385   In all places and at all heights as He was passing,

that same division that was there in the place received Him.

Lightnings accompanied Him and they stayed behind Him at their boundaries,

(as well as) clouds, winds and breezes of the air as He ascended.

The captains and their (heavenly) hosts in their realms

390   received Him and stayed behind Him, being afraid.

Those that are above the intermediary ones received and escorted Him.

And the beings below stayed behind and step by step every legion in its place.

The companies of fiery beings received Him with great trembling;

and they remained back from Him in their regions while trembling.

395   All the heavenly principalities went out to honour Him

but He left them and was raised to the height that is above.

He reached the chariot, however, He did not remain on the chariot,

for above that (chariot) to the extended heights He was being raised.

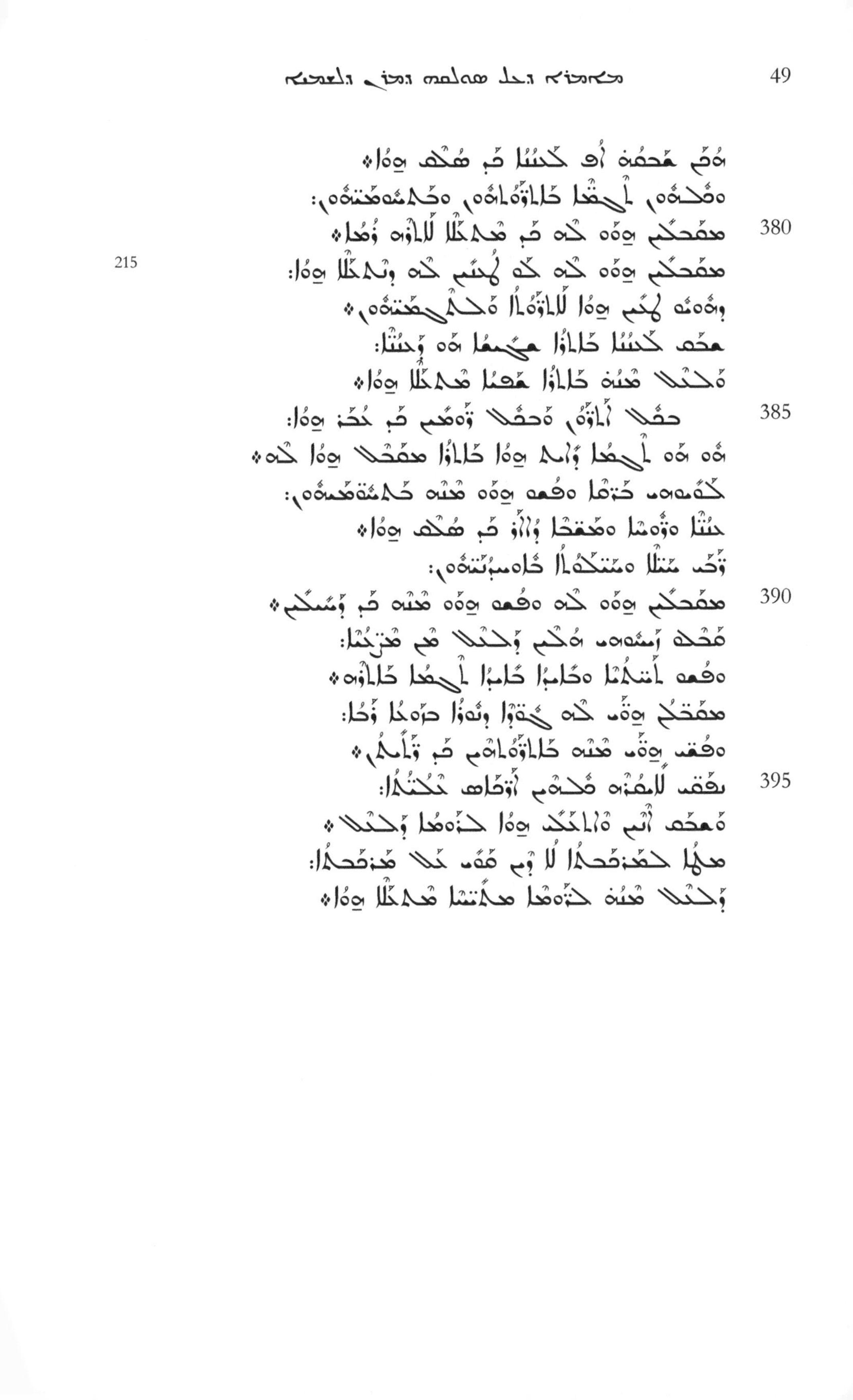

It [*the chariot*] also had received Him in its place as He
    was ascending;

400   and as much as the boundary that was set to it to as-
    cend with Him, it ascended.

And it stayed behind Him and He ascended towards
    His Father

where there is no place for the angels to move for-
    ward.

He left behind the Seraphs who were singing 'Holy,   Isa 6:3
    holy, holy,' with their hallowings.

The fearful Cherubs who were making joyful noise for
    Him with great trembling,

405   Persons and faces as well as wings and wheels en-
    dowed with speech,

the cloud of fire all of which distils flame.

Above these the Only-Begotten bore himself magnifi-
    cently,

to the region where there is no room for the minds to
    be raised up;

To the holy of holies, the High Priest bore himself   Cf. Heb 9:11,
    magnificently,   24

410   because no one has power to enter into it except the
    Only One;

Towards that awesome interior tabernacle where the
    Father is,

for the Son alone can enter towards His Father.

MOUNT SINAI AND THE ORDER OF THE ASCENSION OF THE SON

Outside the door the angels stayed behind like the
    Levites,

and Christ, the High Priest, alone entered.

415   The heavenly hosts, tribes by tribes,

legions by legions, bands by bands (remained) in their
    (different) ranks:

In the valley of the heights they stayed behind Him as   Exod 19:16–25
    He was ascending,

like the Hebrews gathered together around Sinai.

To the top of the mountain no one ascended, but
    Moses,

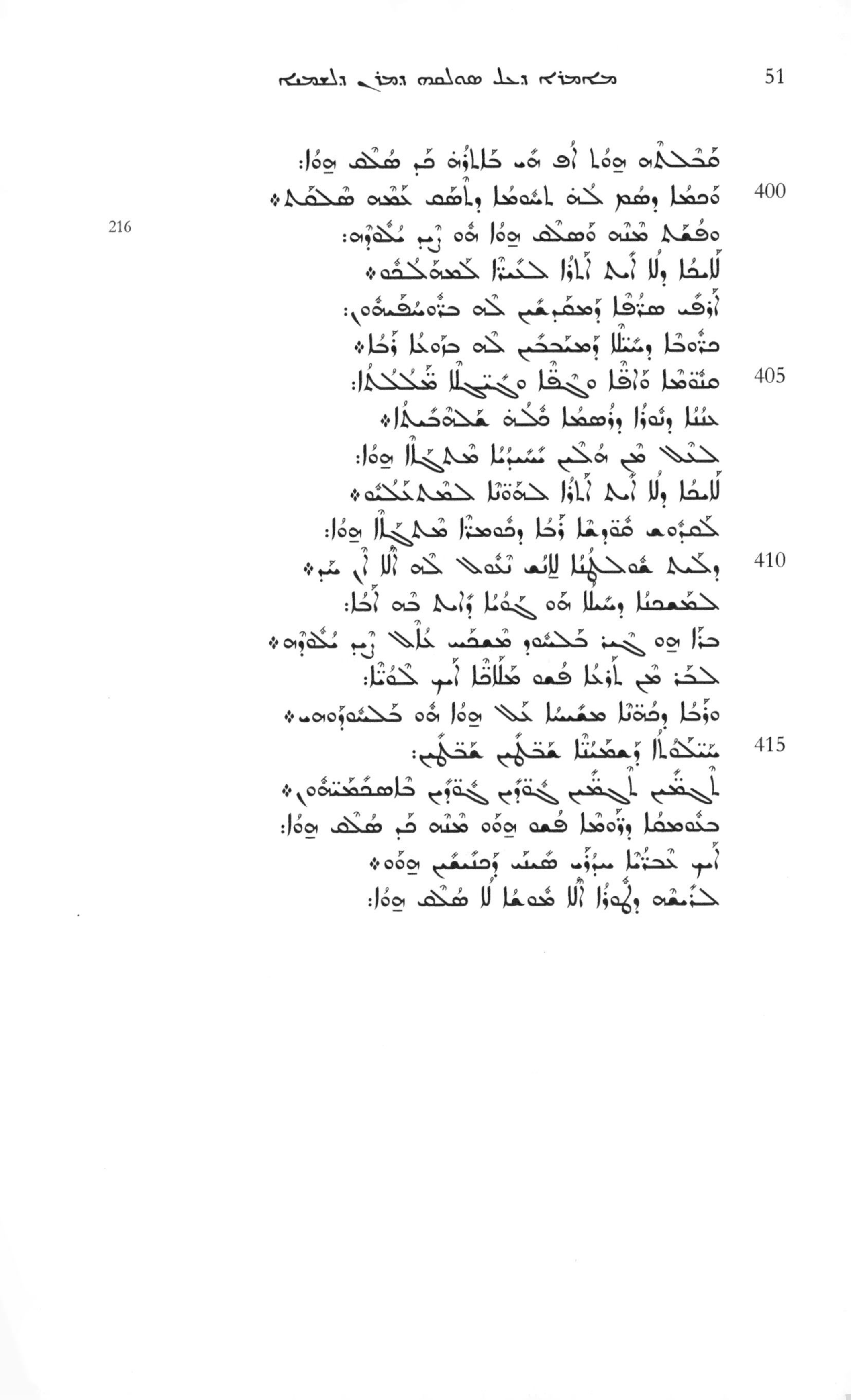

420   but to its intermediary level the elders and the priests
            were raised.
        Around it the people and on its slopes the leaders of
            the people (remained),
        and where there was the tabernacle of the Exalted
            One Moses alone (entered).
        Heaven was full of heavenly armies
        and above them were set up the archangels.
425   And again other heavenly beings who are higher than
            their comrades,
        and as the High Priest, the Son of God, within all
            these.
        To the place where the great Moses ascended
        neither priests nor Levites nor the leaders of the peo-
            ple ascended.
        To the place where the Son was exalted, with His Fa-
            ther,
430   neither Cherubs nor Seraphs with their hallowings
            were raised.
        There are priests but the High Priest is only one;   Cf. Heb 9:7
        and into the holy of holies, only One enters, not
            many.
        The Only-Begotten alone entered to His Father
        and there is no means for another one to enter to the
            Father.

The Entrance of the Son into the Hidden Tabernacle

435   King David, the divine harpist,
        stirred up his voice to the gates of the height to open
            them.
        As if to say, O gates from eternity, be lifted up,   Ps 24:9
        for they are never opened to anyone to enter but for
            Him.
        From that place of the heights, and from that place of
            the gates the angels stayed behind,
440   and the gates were lifted up so that the King alone
            might enter,
        to the region, hidden, concealed, and fearful that can-
            not be spoken of,

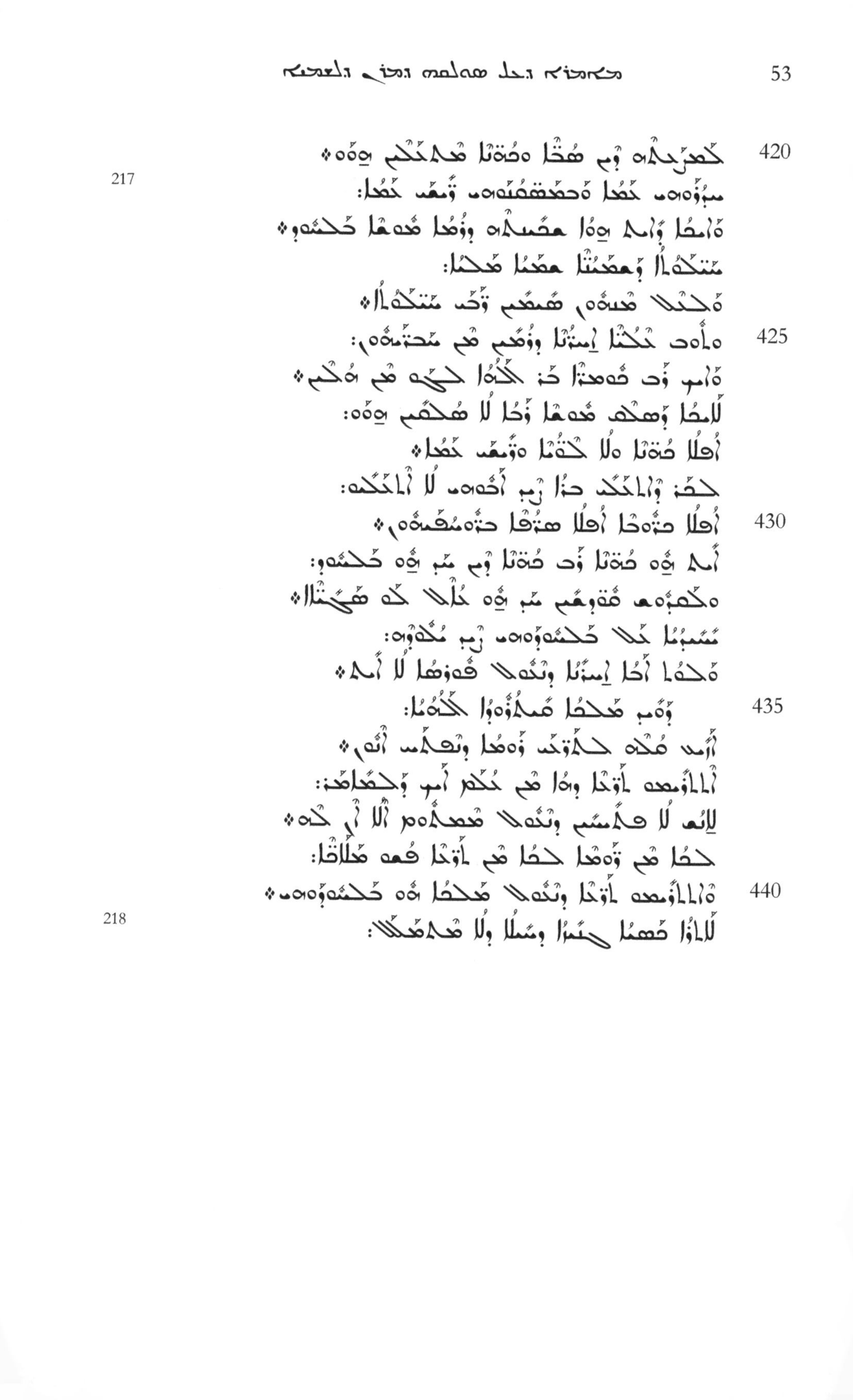

217

218

higher than all heights and lengths and regions.

Legions after legions remained behind Him as He was
    ascending.

Each of them remained in its region but He was ex-
    alted,

445   to the hidden place which is not at all part of creation,

nor is its story mingled with created things and the
    things formed,

The tabernacle which is not made, nor has it any like
    it among created things,

the region far from angels and from human intellects.

Neither minds nor thoughts ascend to it.

450   Nor do they contemplate it, not even the angels can
    speak where it is.

The beings below stayed behind, the intermediaries
    remained behind and the supernal beings

stayed back; and those above them remained within
    the boundary of their realms.

As He was concealed from that company which was   Acts 1:9
    on the Mount of Olives,

He was concealed from the intermediaries and from
    the beings above.

455   And He alone entered into that inner holy of holies

and no one entered with Him, neither intellect nor
    thought.

The mind itself stayed behind Him and it was not able
    to venture

to be raised again to look at the Son (to see) how
    much He was exalted.

Like an angel the mind ascends and it cannot do any
    more.

460   And where the watchers remain, thoughts as well re-
    main.

The Son was veiled from men[26] and from the angels

as He was veiled from Thomas and from John too.

As far as he could gaze, Simon looked on when He
    ascended.

---

[26] Lit., 'minds.'

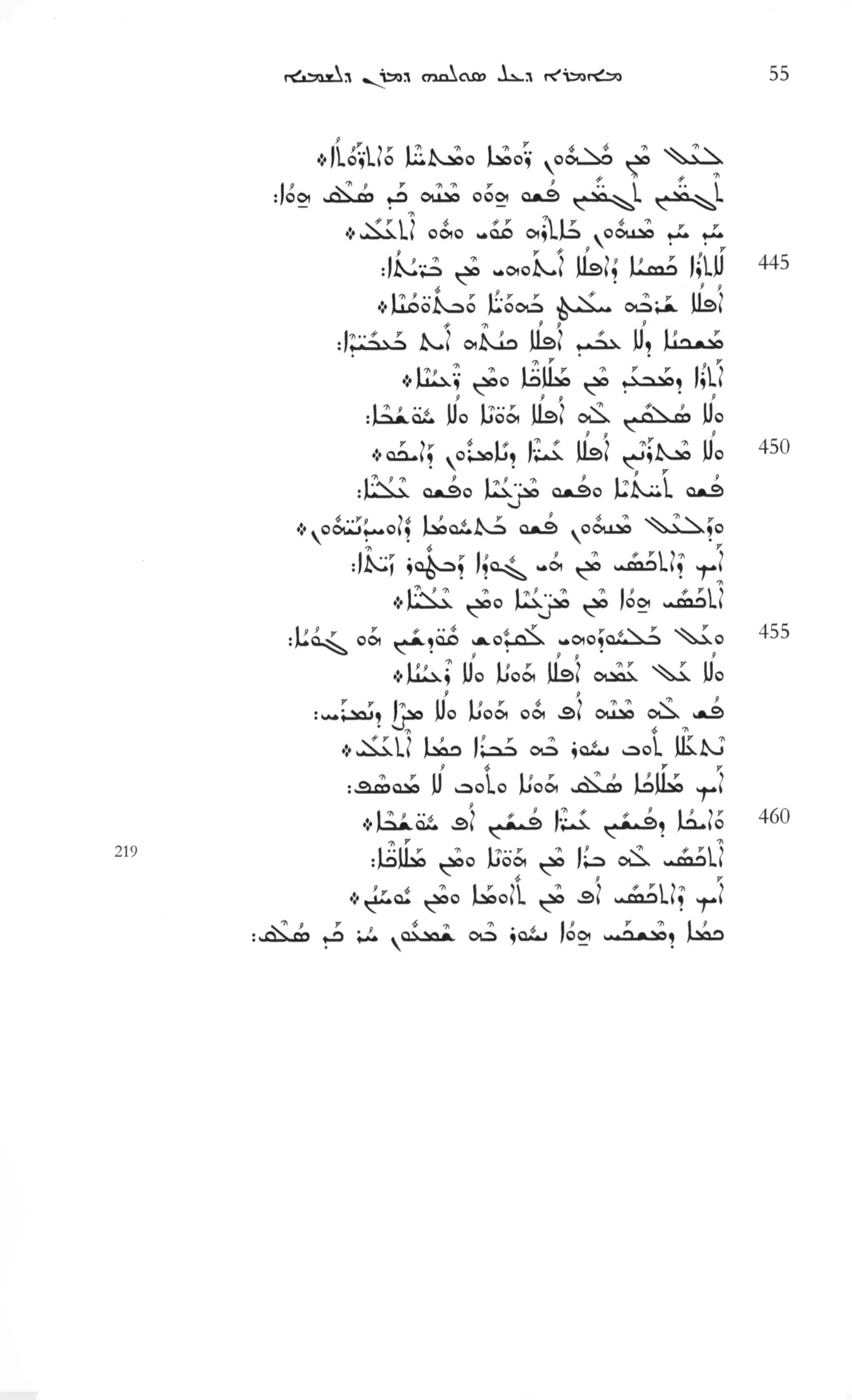

219

As far as he could Gabriel gazed on, and Michael too.
465 And as far as it is able to venture even the mind too
gazed.
The thoughts too extended their impulses to see His
place.
He was exalted, went far in; He was hidden
from the disciples and from the angels, from the intellects too,
And from the minds and from the thoughts and from
their impulses;
470 and they were not able to set about to look on Him
(to see) how far He was exalted.
Stay behind, O Simon, your Lord has ascended to His
exalted place
and as far as you would gaze, you will not see how far
He has been exalted.
Stay behind, O Gabriel, because He has been exalted
above your legion
and you are not empowered to be exalted after Him
to His place.
475 Rest, O Chariot, and move your wheels to speak,
because you are not allowed by the Hidden One in
His place to see His place.
Rest, Michael, O great leader of the heavenly hosts
because you will not reach the high stairs of your
Lord.
Rest yourself, O Intellect, because the one who ven-
tures, advancing and leaping, will fall;
480 so you should not again venture upon the steps which
are incomprehensible.
The High Priest[27] has entered into the holy of holies,
with His own blood He will reconcile His Father with
humanity.
Cf. Col 1:20,
Heb 9:14

---

[27] Cf. Narsai, *Hom. on the Ascension* (PO 40, pp. 167, 175).

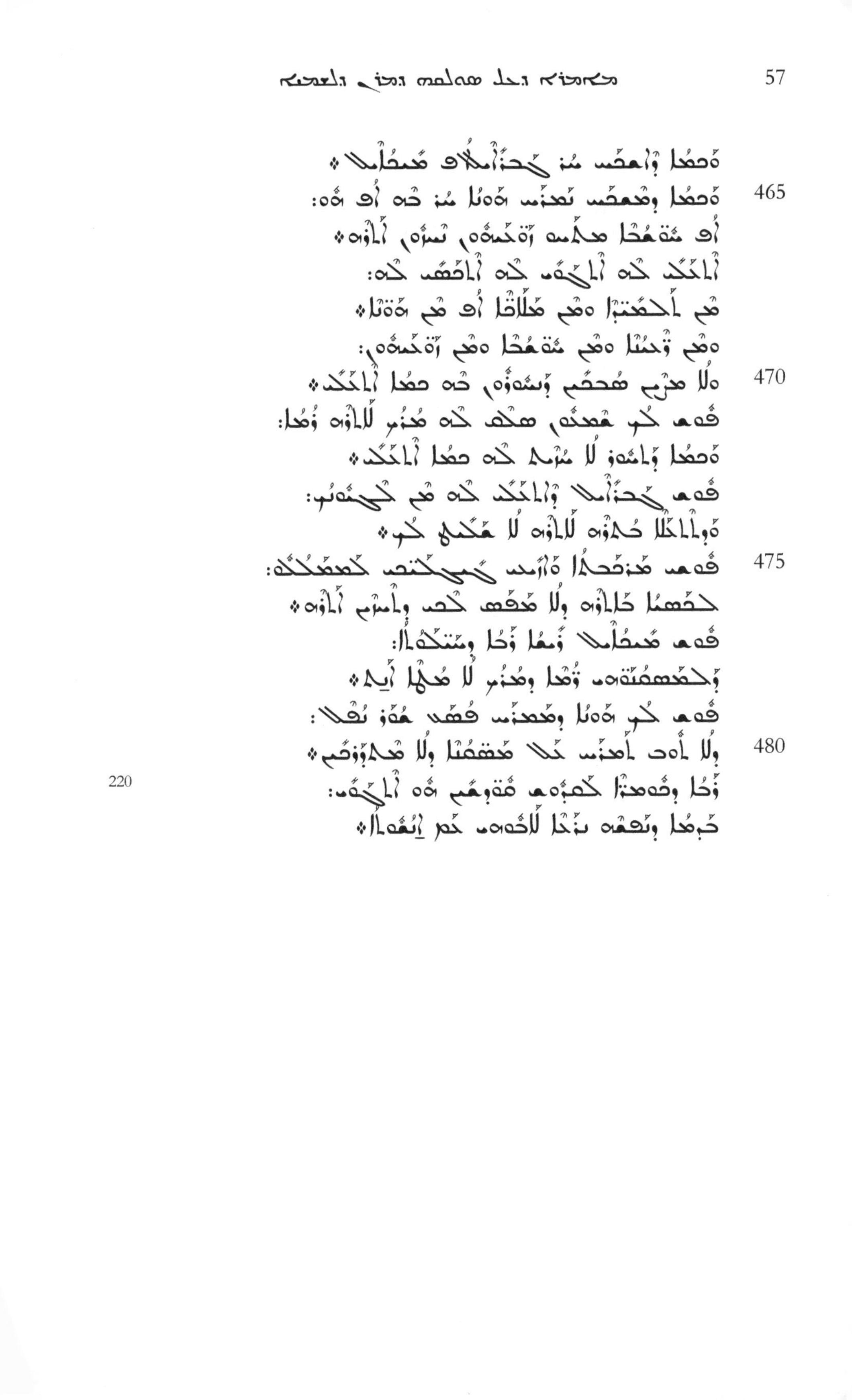

He is the offering, the High Priest, and the libation
  too[28]
and He himself entered so that the whole creation
  might be pardoned through Him.
485   That One who descended, ascended, and that One
  who brought himself low has subdued the
  heights.
He descended, visited us and ascended redeeming us;
  To Him be glory.
The end of the Homily on Ascension.

---

[28] Cf. Bedjan III, p. 259, lines 10–11 (Hom. 78, on the Red Heifer; ET by D. Lane, *The Harp* 15 [2002], 25–42); Bedjan V, p. 158, lines 5–20 (Hom. 155) (Melchizedek is the type of Christ's self-offering); Ephrem *HAzym* 2:2–3,5; *Crucif* 3:10; Narsai, *PO* 40, pp. 166/167 (lines 81–84).

ܘܗܘܐ ܘܚܡܐ ܗܘܙܐ ܘܩܢܠܐ ܐܘ ܢܘܡܠܐ:
ܘܗܘ ܠܗ ܗܢܝܠ ܘܗܘ ܐܡܢܗܐ ܡܟܚ ܚܙܟܐ܀

485 ܡܠܗ ܗܘ ܙܝܫܐ ܘܚܒܡ ܙܘܗܐ ܙܘܗܕܐ ܗܘ ܘܐܠܐܣܟܡ:
ܘܗܘ ܝܫܐ ܗܕܢ ܘܗܘ ܡܠܗ ܩܙܥ ܠܗ ܐܡܚܘܣܟܐ܀

ܡܠܡ ܘܢܠܐ ܦܘܠܟܡܐ.

BIBLIOGRAPHY OF WORKS CITED

(A) SYRIAC AUTHORS

Jacob:

Albert, *Juifs* = M. Albert, *Homélies contre les juifs par Jacques de Sarough* (PO 38:1, 1976).

Bedjan I-VI = *Hom. Selectae Mar-Jacobi Sarugensis* I-V (Paris/Leipzig, 1905–1910; reprinted with extra vol. VI, Piscataway NJ, 2006).

Kollamparampil, *Festal Homilies* = T. Kollamparampil, *Jacob of Serugh. Select Festal Homilies* (Rome/Bangalore, 1997).

Kollamparampil, T., *Jacob of Sarug's Homily on Palm Sunday* (MHMJS 3; Piscataway NJ, 2008).

_____, *Jacob of Sarug's Homily on the Transfiguration of our Lord* (MHMJS 8; Piscataway NJ , 2008).

_____, *Jacob of Sarug's Homily on the Presentation in the Temple* (MHMJS ?; Piscataway NJ, 200?).

D. Lane, 'Jacob of Sarug, on the Red Heifer', *The Harp* 15 (2002), 25–42.

Turgome = F. Rilliet, *Jacques de Saroug. Homélies festales en prose* (PO 43:4; 1986).

Ephrem:

Ephrem, *Comm. Diatessaron* = L. Leloir, *Saint Éphrem, Commentaire de l'Évangile concordant* (Dublin, 1963); *Folios Additionels*: Leuven, 1990).

_____, *HAzym* = *Hymni de Azymis*, in *Des heiligen Ephraem des Syrers Paschahymnen* (ed. E. Beck, CSCO 248–9 = Scr. Syri 108–9; 1964).

_____, *HCruc* = *Hymni de Crucifixione*, in *Des heiligen Ephraem des Syrers Paschahymnen* (ed. E. Beck, CSCO 248–9 = Scr. Syri 109–9; 1964).

_____, *HEccl* = *Des heiligen Ephraem des Syrers Hymnen de Ecclesia* (ed. E. Beck, CSCO 198–9 = Scr. Syri 84–5; 1960).

_____, *HFid* = *Des heiligen Ephraem des Syrers Hymnen de Fide* (ed. E. Beck, CSCO 154–5 = Scr/ Syri 73–4; 1955).

_____, *CNis* = *Des heiligen Ephraem des Syrers Carmina Nisibena* I-II (ed. E. Beck, CSCO 218–9, 240–1 = Scr. Syri 92–3, 102–3; 1961, 1963).

_____, *HPar* = *Des heiligen Ephraem des Syrers Hymnen de Paradiso und contra Julianum* (ed. E. Beck, CSCO 174–5 = Scr. Syri 78–9; 1957).

_____, *HRes* = *Des heiligen Ephraem des Syrers Paschahymnen* (ed. E. Beck, CSCO 248–9 = Scr. Syri 108–9; 1964).

Narsai:

F. G. McLeod, *Narsai's Metrical Homilies on the Nativity, Epiphany, Passion, Resurrection and Ascension* (PO 40:1; 1979).

(B) MODERN LITERATURE

S. P. Brock, *The Luminous Eye. The Spiritual World View of St Ephrem* (Kalamazoo, 1992).

T. Kollamparampil, *Salvation in Christ according to Jacob of Serugh* (Bangalore, 2001).

INDEX OF NAMES AND THEMES

INDEX OF BIBLICAL REFERENCES